FATHER SCOTT'S RADIO TALKS

1927-1928

STATION WLWL

Other Books by the Same Author

CHRIST OR CHAOS
CONVENT LIFE
GOD AND MYSELF
THE HAND OF GOD
YOU AND YOURS
RELIGION AND COMMON SENSE
THE DIVINE COUNSELLOR
CREDENTIALS OF CHRISTIANITY
ISAAC JOGUES, MISSIONER AND MARTYR
THE HOLY SACRIFICE OF THE MASS
THINGS CATHOLICS ARE ASKED ABOUT

FATHER SCOTT'S RADIO TALKS

1927–1928

STATION WLWL

BY

MARTIN J. SCOTT, S.J.

NEW YORK
P. J. KENEDY & SONS
1928

Imprimi Potest:

EDWARD C. PHILLIPS, S.J.

Præpositus, Prov. Marylandiæ Neo-Eboracensis

Nihil Obstat:

ARTHUR J. SCANLAN, S.T.D.

Censor Librorum

Imprimatur:

✠ PATRICK CARDINAL HAYES

Archbishop, New York

New York
October 18, 1928.

Printed in the United States of America

To

MICHAEL J. JORDAN

PRESIDENT OF
THE CATHOLIC ALUMNI SODALITY,
BOSTON COLLEGE,
WHOSE RARE SCHOLARSHIP
HAS BEEN GENEROUSLY DEVOTED TO
THE CAUSE OF HOLY MOTHER CHURCH,
THIS VOLUME IS DEDICATED
WITH THE ESTEEM AND AFFECTION OF
THE AUTHOR

CONTENTS

PREFACE

IN presenting in book-form the talks which he gave over the Paulist Radio Station WLWL, the author is yielding to a wide-spread request for their publication. These radio talks, which created great interest and most favorable comment, are now given to the public in permanent form. It is hoped that they will be as desirable in print as they were on the air.

The keen interest at present displayed in things Catholic, makes it advisable to be well-informed on what so much concerns people generally. It is hoped that these talks will serve to make the True Religion better known and revered, not only by those of the Faith, but also by those whom misinformation or environment has kept aloof from the truth. If the true Church of Christ be rightly known she will be revered by all who are open to conviction.

FATHER SCOTT'S RADIO TALKS

1927-1928

CHAPTER I

DOES IT MATTER WHAT WE BELIEVE?

IT is not uncommon to hear people say that it is not what you believe that matters, but what you do. Undoubtedly it is what you do that matters; but what you do depends mostly on what you believe. If you believe that it is right to steal you will most likely become a thief. Anarchists believe it is right to assassinate in order to promote a cause; so they commit murder without hesitation. Socialists believe that it is right to equalize resources; so they confiscate private property as we see in Soviet Russia. Cannibals believe it is right to kill human beings and eat them; so they kill and eat captives.

You may say that these are extreme or abnormal cases. But this only shows that wrong beliefs lead to extreme and unnatural conduct. A merchant who believes that it is right to burn his store and stock of goods to get the insurance; or to fail, in order to enrich himself by bankruptcy, will act on his beliefs. It is because so many people have wrong principles of conduct and business that crime and dishonesty are so widespread at present.

Beliefs are principles of action. If a man's business or personal conduct rests on false principles he becomes a menace to others and eventually the cause of ruin to himself. There are those who believe that liberty means license to do as one wills. Such people ride roughshod over civil and social customs and laws. Some people mistake independence for lawlessness thus becoming a law to themselves and a danger to the community. So it does matter what we believe.

The Constitution of the United States is a document which expresses our belief on political matters. Will anyone say that the Constitution does not matter? For nearly two hundred years it has directed the destinies of our country. The Monroe Doctrine is another of our political beliefs. This Doctrine has dictated our foreign policy for a century. It matters so much that to uphold it our Government would go to war. The Constitution of the United States is our political doctrine or dogma. We know that it not only matters, but matters so much that without it we should not long be able to survive as a nation. The Civil War was waged to uphold the Constitution. The legion of lives and the millions of treasure which it cost attest that belief does matter.

Belief, doctrine, principle and *dogma* mean very much the same. As I shall use the word *dogma* frequently in discussing this matter, let me say that *dogma* means *doctrine* or *teaching*. It is a statement of belief or principles.

As dogma matters in social and political life, so does it matter in religion. For instance: it is a dogma of Christianity that the soul of man is immortal. It makes a great difference whether we are made for time or eternity. If this present life terminate forever my career I will live for this life only. The only thing that will influence my conduct will be its bearing on my welfare in this life. If I believe that there is no future retribution I shall take into account present consequences only. My motto will be: "Eat, drink and be merry, for to-morrow we die." Or as the pagan poet puts it: "The flower that once has blown forever dies."

There are many things that I would do if I believed that this life ended my career, which I would not do if I believed that the grave is not the goal but starting point of man. The dogma of the immortality of the soul is thus seen to be a very serious matter. In point of fact a great majority of the host of criminals which now infest our own and other countries are men who either do not believe in future judgment or whose belief is nominal only. A dogma, like everything else, must be seriously believed in order to be effective. No principle of conduct will influence those who have it on their lips, but not in their heart. The Monroe Doctrine would never have directed our international policy if it were merely a nominal creed. When, therefore, we say that it matters what we believe we mean if we seriously believe.

If a man believe in the Ten Commandments his life will be different from one who does not believe in them. It is because so many people have recently been carried away by materialistic belief that we have the morals of the jungle in modern life. If I am only a high-grade animal, as some advocates of evolution contend, why should I not gratify my animal passions and instincts? And this is what many so-called enlightened people are doing, with the result that morals have in many respects degenerated to the animal level. Lust, strength and cunning have replaced the law of God. In consequence the stage has become a panderer to passion, business is honeycombed with dishonesty, life is held cheap, perjury brazenly defies the law, and lust challenges us even in the street. No wonder that conservative men of all creeds are becoming alarmed for the future.

Russia is governed to-day by the dogma that there is no God, no hereafter. The condition of Russia is clearest evidence that it does matter what we believe. There, by control of the army and revenue, a few men make slaves of a nation. They are simply translating their dogma into action. The Bolsheviks are examples of men whose belief is real not nominal.

I might go on indefinitely to show that it is absolutely false to assert that it does not matter what we believe. But I think I have said sufficient to convince those who are open to conviction, that belief, or dogma, not only matters but is of paramount importance. It is for this reason that the Church of Christ holds dogma so sacred. The dogma or teaching of Christianity is the doctrine of life which her Divine Founder committed to His Church. We revere the Constitution which, after all, is but the work of man. The dogmas of Christianity are the teaching of Jesus Christ, the Son of God. This is why a real believer in Christ's religion is willing to die rather than to deny by word or deed the dogmas of the Church. The teaching of men, even of the wisest men, may or may not be true. But the teaching of Christ is as true as God. Jesus said of Himself: "I am the Way, and the Truth, and the Life. . . . I am the Light of the World. . . . He who followeth after Me walketh not in darkness."

A Christian is a follower of Christ, a believer that Christ is God. Hence for the dogmas of Christ's Church he will, if need be, sacrifice his life. A believer in Christ realizes that the Master has said: "He that shall lose his life for My sake, shall find it." (Mt. xvii. 25.) In consequence of this a true Christian will reverence and observe God's law even at the cost of possessions, liberty or life. Perhaps an example will demonstrate better than words, that it does matter what we believe.

Sir Thomas More was the most celebrated and honored man in the realm of Henry VIII. His power was next to that of the king himself. He had everything except the crown. Henry, knowing the weight of his influence with the people, hoped that if he could get the approval of More for his divorce the whole kingdom would acquiesce. Accordingly he employed every means in his power to get his chancellor to approve of the divorce. He heaped new honors on him, made all sorts of promises to him, and in every way possible sought to win him over.

Finally, when promises and favors failed, he employed threats. He threw More into prison and threatened him with death. But always the chancellor remained firm. The king sent various persons to him to persuade him, but of no avail. The king himself visited him and accused him of stubbornness and ingratitude. More's reply was: "My Lord King, I have but one life; it is very dear to me, but I would gladly give it any time for Your Majesty. If I had two souls I would gladly give one for you; but as I have but one soul, it belongs to God, who purchased it by His passion and death. Rather than lose my soul, I am ready to lose my life. But all else, Sire, that I have is at your command."

Henry, knowing the high esteem in which More was held, hesitated to order him to the block. He tried one last device before committing official murder. More had a daughter, Margaret, whom he loved as seldom father loves child. Her love for him was as great as his for her. There is nothing in human annals more tender than More's love for his daughter Margaret. The king had her sent to her father in prison to prevail on him to come over to his side on the divorce. In tears Margaret pleaded with her beloved father. Only a loving parent can understand the anguish of More under this ordeal.

Finally he said to her: "Well, daughter, suppose I do go over to the king, what then?" "Oh, father," she replied, "he would restore all your honors. Again you would be the first personage in the realm." "And how long, daughter, would I enjoy these honors?" "For years and years. You are young yet. We should have many happy years together in comfort and honor." "How many, daughter?" "Twenty; forty; maybe more." "And after that, daughter?" She made no reply. Instead, tears blinded her as she sobbed: "You are right, darling father. Eternity is too great a price to pay for even the greatest worldly pleasure and honor."

The next day Sir Thomas More was led to the scaffold. Before placing his head on the block, he indulged in pleasantry with the executioner. Running his finger over the edge of the axe he said: "It's a sharp remedy, but a cure for all human ills." The next moment he calmly placed his head on the block, telling the axeman to take good aim and make a clean job of it. The axe fell, and the noblest head in England was severed from its body. The axe fell, and More's mortal life was ended. But his immortal life began. No longer a subject of a monarch of earth, he became a child of God. Blessed Thomas More made the supreme sacrifice. He gave the greatest proof of fidelity and love. God can not be outdone in generosity. For all eternity More will rejoice in that home which God has prepared for them that love Him.

We may not be called upon, as was Sir Thomas More, to confess Christ in our blood. We may not be required to die for Christ, but we are required to live for Him. We may not have the occasion that this martyr had to show his love for Christ, but we all have the opportunity of showing our love for Christ. "If you love Me," He said, "keep My commandments." (Jn. xiv. 15.) This is within the reach of all of us.

Does it matter what we believe? The countless saints who have been made partakers of heavenly happiness by believing in Christ and living their belief attest that it does matter what we believe. But the belief that matters is real, not nominal. The belief that matters is that which influences our lives. Catholic belief, if lived up to, will make for our peace and welfare here and for our eternal welfare hereafter.

CHAPTER II

FAITH

FAITH has various meanings. We speak of having faith in the government, faith in the courts, faith in a friend. A soldier has faith in a military commander; a patient has faith in a physician; a merchant has faith in a policy. We virtually live by faith. Every time we board a train we have faith in the engineer; when we have a prescription filled we have faith in the druggist; when we read of past events we have faith in the historian. If we eliminated faith from our lives we should be at a standstill.

It is not until we reflect that we realize how much of our life depends on faith. Pupils have faith in their teachers; children in their parents; clients in their lawyer. Yet the faith we have in others, whether it be in equals or superiors, is liable to be misplaced. It is human to err. The best human authority or institution may fail those who trust in it. Yet we go on trusting in people and things. We must go on trusting or cease to live normally.

When we have faith in God we put our trust in One Who can not fail us. God can neither deceive nor be deceived. We call faith in God *divine faith.* It means that relying on His goodness and promises we live as He directs. We Catholics speak of our religion as Our Holy Faith. It is also termed Divine Faith because it is based on God's word. If we have faith in a man we rely on his word. In proportion as we have faith in him we believe in him. Divine faith means that we so trust in God that we believe Him absolutely. The mere fact that He has spoken is sufficient warrant for belief. His word is the best argument for the truth of what He says. Divine faith therefore means absolute, unwavering faith in the word of God. It means belief in God's declaration, not because He proves it but because He has spoken. His word is of itself guarantee of the truth of what He says.

The word of a scientist is taken even though what he states be beyond demonstration to the majority of his hearers. Not one person out of a thousand is able to verify the assertions of specialists in various departments of knowledge; yet because of the faith they have in these experts they accept their assertion on their word only. Faith in God means the acceptance of what He says, simply because He has said it. We do not understand many things that God has revealed to us, but we believe them on His word only. The apostle St. John says: "If we receive the testimony of men, the testimony of God is greater." (I Jn. v. 9.)

Divine faith, therefore, means believing what God has declared, not because He has demonstrated the truth of His declarations, but solely because He Who is Truth Itself has made the declaration. Once we demand *the reasons why* from God we cease to regard Him with the absolute trust which characterizes faith, and which is necessary for faith. We may demand *the reason why* from our fellow men, who are our equals; but not of God Who is not only our Sovereign Lord but also the Eternal Truth.

It may be said that all this is quite evident. No one would doubt God's word if God really had spoken to mankind. But that is just the point. Has God spoken to man? Has God revealed to us truths which otherwise we should not know? The answer to this all-important question is given to us by Holy Scripture itself. "God, Who, at sundry times and in divers manners, spoke in times past to the fathers by the prophets, last of all, in these days hath spoken to us by His Son." (Heb. i. 1.)

It was in order that we might know that He was the true Son of God, that Christ performed deeds which God alone could do. He realized that in saying that He was the Son of God, He was making the most stupendous claim ever heard on this earth. But His deeds were in harmony with His claims. By a word only He gave sight to the blind, cleansed the leper, made the cripple to walk and the deaf to hear. As in the beginning God said "Let there be light, and light was made," so Jesus said to the man born blind "Receive thy sight"; and to the leper "I will, be thou made clean"; and to the cripple "Take up thy bed and walk." And the blind saw, and the leper was healed, and the cripple was made whole. Jesus said to the dead son of the widow of Naim: "Young man, I say to thee arise." And the corpse became a man again in response to the voice which in the beginning had said: "Let us make man." (Gen. i. 26.)

St. John tells us: "Many other signs also did Jesus in the sight of His disciples, which are not written in this book. But these are written, that you may believe that Jesus is the Christ, the Son of God: and that believing, you may have life in His name." (Jn. xx. 30, 31.)

In order that we may understand that Jesus is the Son of God, in the sense that He is the true Son of the Eternal God, and that He is in all things equal to the Creator, let us hear the testimony of St. John. Before we give the inspired words of the apostle, let it be remarked that when philosophers and Scripture employ the term *Word* with reference to The Deity it means The Power by which the world was made. St. John, speaking of Jesus and applying this term to Him, speaks as follows in the sublime opening passage of his Gospel: "In the beginning was the Word, and the Word was with God, and the Word was God . . . all things were made by Him . . . and the Word was made flesh, and dwelt among us." (Jn. i. 1, 14.) Jesus is therefore the Son of God become man. He is God in the true sense. He is the Creator and Lord of the World. Jesus, the true Son of God, has spoken to us.

Faith in Jesus is therefore faith in God; when Jesus speaks, God speaks. What Jesus has revealed, that God has revealed. It was for this reason that St. Paul, in his Epistle to the Thessalonians, says: "We give thanks to God without ceasing: because, that when you had received of us the word of the hearing of God, you received it not as the word of men, but (as it is indeed) the word of God." (I Thes. ii. 13.) The apostles were not preaching their own doctrine but that of Jesus, and they proclaimed that what they preached was the word of God.

The same apostle emphasizes this fact when, addressing the Galatians, he says: "I give you to understand, that the Gospel which was preached by me is not according to man: for neither did I receive it of man, nor did I learn it; but by the revelation of Jesus Christ." (Gal. i. 11, 12.) God, therefore, has spoken to man. As true as that Christ is God, so true is it that God has spoken to man.

We should use our reason and every means at our disposal to know if Jesus be God. But once we believe in the divinity of Jesus Christ we must believe that when He speaks, God speaks. We may, if we will, deny that there is a God, or that Christ is God; but we cannot believe that Christ is God without believing that God has spoken to us.

All Christians believe that Christ is God. All Christians therefore believe that God has spoken to man. *Christian Faith* therefore means believing what Jesus Christ has revealed, because He has revealed it. It does not mean that we understand how the matter revealed is so—as, for instance, the mystery of the Trinity—but that we believe the fact on the word of God Who has declared it. Christians do not believe because they commend or admire the teaching of Jesus, but because they believe that He is God and that what He teaches is true.

Christian Faith does not permit our choosing to accept only what we like of the teaching of Jesus. We must accept all or reject all. God can not be partly true and partly false. What He teaches is therefore all true. Divine Faith does not permit of selecting the doctrines which appeal to us and rejecting what does not appeal to us. That is not faith in Christ, but in ourselves.

In brief, Faith is not subjective nor sentimental nor selective. Faith is the acceptance and firm belief in all that Christ teaches because He teaches it. Some people who call themselves Christians believe certain parts of the Gospel but not other parts. In doing that they are making their own religion, but it is not Christ's religion. Christ's religion is definite and unchangeable. Truth never changes. Truth can not contradict itself.

The dissensions so deplorable among non-Catholic denominations come from a false notion of Faith. Every non-Catholic denomination owes its origin to personal or subjective views. If Christ taught a body of truths He was certainly not indifferent to their acceptance. He did not leave them to be taken or rejected at the judgment of the individual. To say that God would guide each one what to believe after God Himself had specified what to believe is to stultify God. Moreover, God can not inspire contradictory beliefs. He gave to mankind a definite Creed, so sacred and fixed and perpetual that St. Paul said of it: "Though we, or an angel from heaven, preach a gospel to you besides that which we have preached to you, let him be anathema." (Gal. i. 8.)

Outside the Catholic Church new creeds are being made every day by those calling themselves Christians. These are man-made religions. There is only one Creed in the world that is not man-made and that is the Creed which has come down to us from the apostles who received it from Jesus Christ, the Son of God: "I believe in God, the Father Almighty, Creator of heaven and earth; and in Jesus Christ, His only Son, our Lord, Who was conceived by the Holy Ghost, born of the Virgin Mary, suffered under Pontius Pilate, was crucified, died, and was buried; He descended into hell; the third day He rose again from the dead; He ascended into heaven, sitteth at the right hand of God, the Father Almighty; from thence He shall come to judge the living and the dead. I believe in the

Holy Ghost; the Holy Catholic Church; the communion of saints; the forgiveness of sins; the resurrection of the body; and life everlasting. Amen." (Apostles' Creed.)

CHAPTER III

MODERNISM

AT present we hear a great deal about modernism. Pulpit, press and platform resound with discussions on political, social and religious modernism. What is modernism? Let me begin by saying that the word *modernism* is not happily chosen to designate what it stands for. Some people might think that those who oppose modernism are opposed to modern progress. But this is far from being the case.

Modernism, as a term at present applied to religious matters, designates a movement which is subversive of the principles and practices of Christianity. Modernism in religion is a revolt against authority. It is the substitution of personal views for authoritative and divine teaching. It means the denial of Christian dogma as promulgated once for all by Jesus Christ the divine Founder of the Christian religion. Modernism logically carried out would destroy Christianity. In brief, the purpose of modernism in religion is to change the unchangeable truth revealed by Christ, and make it conform to modern tendencies, instead of making these tendencies conform to the eternal truth revealed to mankind by Jesus Christ the Way, the Truth, and the Life.

Modernism would strip Jesus Christ and His revelation of their supernatural character and reduce the Christian religion to the level of a system of philosophy. But Christianity is not a school of philosophy. It is the eternal truth proclaimed to mankind by God Himself. Christianity is a divine command. Christianity is the Voice of the Ruler of the World proclaiming His ordinances to mankind.

There have been wise men and philosophers before and after Christ. These sages proposed systems of thought and conduct and gave arguments to show that their principles were reasonable. They were men speaking to men, arguing with men, endeavoring to convince men. Their systems of thought and conduct had no authority to oblige mankind to accept them. The various schools of philosophy and morality were speculative, persuasive, and argumentative.

Not so the teaching of Jesus Christ the Eternal Son of God. His teaching was not speculative. It was divine truth. He did not explain His doctrine nor argue about it. He commanded mankind to accept it under penalty of incurring divine chastisement for refusal. He first demonstrated by divine deeds that He was what He proclaimed Himself to be, the Creator and Ruler of the World, and then demanded the same respect for and obedience to His doctrine which should be shown to the commands of God Almighty.

Christ knew He was making the most tremendous claims ever made in this world, and consequently made it clear that He was what He declared Himself to be, by presenting divine credentials for His mission. He said: "If you do not believe Me, at least believe the works which I do." (Jn. x. 38.) He gave sight to the blind, made the lame to walk, cleansed the leper, raised the dead to life, and foretold the future. After thus demonstrating that He was God in the true sense—the Creator of the World, Jehovah—He spoke with the authority and power of God. He never explained His doctrine but only proclaimed it, as was befitting God. He wanted to be obeyed as God, not argued with as man. Hence He did not explain His doctrine but proclaimed it.

Christ did not explain the Trinity, but proclaimed it, commanding His Church to baptize in the name of the Father, and of the Son, and of the Holy Ghost. (Mt. xxviii. 19.) He did not explain the Incarnation but solemnly proclaimed that He was the Eternal Son of the Eternal Father. He did not explain how He should give mankind His Body and Blood as food and drink, but proclaimed: "Except you eat the flesh of the Son of Man, and drink His blood, you shall not have life in you." (Jn. vi. 54.) When some of His followers left Him because this was hard of belief, He did not retract nor explain, but repeated the doctrine with emphasis. At the Last Supper He instituted the Blessed Eucharist as the means by which He was to give Himself to His lovers. But He did not explain the mystery of the Eucharist.

St. Augustine declared that he would not believe that the Christian religion was divine if it did not proclaim mysteries. The fact that Christ taught what is above human comprehension shows that He is more than man. The fact that He imposed His doctrine on mankind shows that He is God. All through His mission He spoke as God, He acted as God, He demanded to be believed as God.

Christianity, therefore, is not a system of philosophy. Christianity is a divine command to mankind. It is the will of the Ruler of the Universe declared to His rational creatures—mankind. Christ did not propose His teaching for debate, He imposed it for acceptance, solely on His divine authority. Christ spoke with power. The Jews observed this, and said: "Never did man speak like this man." (Jn. vii. 46.) And again, after the Sermon on the Mount, the Gospel states: "And it came to pass when Jesus had fully ended these words, the people were in admiration at His doctrine. For He was teaching them as one having power, and not as the Scribes and Pharisees." (Mt. vii. 28, 29.)

Unless Jesus was a Divine Teacher He was an impostor. If Jesus was a Divine Teacher what He taught was true when He taught it, true now, and will be true always. Men cannot improve on God. Truth never changes. Two plus two made four in the beginning, and will make four to the end. Because mathematics do not change, that does not mean that they are opposed to progress. All the progress in the mechanical and material world is based on the stability of mathematics.

Not only does truth not change but human nature does not change. Man's passions and tendencies to-day are just what they were when Christ gave His revelation to mankind. Man's environment may change. There may be more material comforts in the world to-day than in the time of Christ but the heart of man is the very same.

Christ instituted His religion for mankind for all time. When He established His Church He gave her a mission that was to last until the end of the world, and moreover promised to abide with her forever. "Going, therefore, teach ye all nations . . . teaching them to observe all things whatsoever I have commanded you: and behold I am with you all days, even till the consummation of the world." (Mt. xxviii. 19, 20.) Jesus Who spoke these words was the Eternal Son of the Eternal Father. He gave to His Church the very same mission that the Almighty Father had entrusted to Himself. "I came forth from the Father, and am come into the world: again I leave the world, and go to the Father." (Jn. xvi. 28.) "As the Father hath sent Me, I also send you." (Jn. xx. 21.) "Go ye into the whole world, and preach the Gospel to every creature." (Mk. xvi. 15.) By this divine authorization Christ commissioned His Church to continue to the end of time the ministry He had inaugurated during His stay on earth.

Christianity is the only religion in the world which has divine credentials and modern historical evidence for its origin. As we know, Christ is the turning point of history. We specify our years as B.C., which means before Christ; or A.D., which means after Christ, or the year of Our Lord. Modern history begins with Christ. The divine Founder of Christianity lived and established His Church in a period of the world's history which is known as the golden age of literature. It was the era of Caesar and Tacitus and Pliny. The events of Christ's life are better authenticated than those of Caesar or Augustus. Harnack, the high-priest of rationalism, has declared that no scholar may reasonably doubt the genuineness of the Gospels. The Gospels are historical documents of the highest authority. If we reject the Gospels we must reject every record of the past. Christ and His Church are therefore facts of history.

If Christ be not God He is the most criminal and sacrilegious impostor that this world has known. He solemnly proclaimed that He was God. And He meant God in the true sense, because He affirmed that He was the Author of Life, that He was Eternal, and that He was equal to the Father in all things. The Jews understood Him to mean that He was God in the true sense—that is, that He was Jehovah. For that reason they declared that He was a blasphemer because He said that Almighty God was

His Father and that He was equal to Him in all things.

He was crucified because He solemnly proclaimed that He was true God. The high-priest said to Jesus: "Art Thou the Christ the Son of the blessed God? And Jesus said to Him: I am. And you shall see the Son of Man sitting on the right hand of the power of God, and coming with the clouds of heaven. Then the high-priest rending his garments, saith: What need we of any further witnesses? You have heard the blasphemy. What think you? Who all condemned Him to be guilty of death." (Mk. xiv. 61-64.) Unless they understood Christ to mean that He was true God they would not have accused Him of blasphemy.

St. Matthew makes it very clear that Christ proclaimed Himself true God: "And the high-priest said to Jesus: I adjure Thee by the living God, that Thou tell us if Thou be the Christ the Son of God?" (Mt. xxvi. 63.) Christ was thus put under oath and solemnly declared that He was the true Son of the living God. Christ is therefore either God or a blasphemer. We know that He is God.

It was Christ the Son of God Who founded the Christian Church. Christ taught the truth and only the truth. He commissioned His

Church to do the same, and gave His divine guarantee that she should always teach the truth He had imparted to her. He commanded mankind to obey the Church as they should obey Him: "He that heareth you, heareth Me." (Lk. x. 16.)

Modernists may be modernists if they wish, but they cannot be modernists and Christians. They may label themselves Christian, but in reality they are members not of Christ's Church but of their own Church. Christ's Church is as authoritative and true as Christ Himself. Modernists in rejecting authoritative religion reject Christianity.

There is but one Church in the world which speaks with the authority and certainty of Christ, and that is the authoritative and infallible Church established by Christ Himself and with which He promised to abide forever. No Church that does not speak infallibly and authoritatively may reasonably claim to be the Church of Christ. The Catholic Church is authoritative and infallible. The Catholic Church goes back directly to Christ. The Catholic Church is the Church established by Jesus Christ the Son of God.

CHAPTER IV

CHURCH UNITY

BEFORE I begin the subject of this evening's talk, I wish to thank those of various denominations who have written to me in commendation of the matter and manner of my radio talks. Knowing that my invisible audience may number those of all creeds and of no creed, my purpose is to avoid controversy, from which good results seldom come. I have always felt that the best argument for truth is its plain statement.

The better the Catholic Church is known the more she appeals to those who are open to conviction. Too often those who think they know the Catholic Church know only a caricature of her. The more light thrown upon her the more she shows divine. She fears but one thing—namely, ignorance of her. Many who assailed her have, with deeper knowledge of her, become her champions. In this respect it may not be uninteresting to you to be informed that one-fourth of all the Catholic priests in England to-day are former Protestant ministers. When we realize that all these scholarly men were obliged to make great sacrifices in order to leave the Church of their life-long association, we may understand that the Catholic Church when known for what she is, and not for what she is too often caricatured, stands the light of historic and scientific investigation as does no other Church in the world.

After this too long preamble let me come to the topic of the evening.

The recent Encyclical of the Holy Father on Church Unity has aroused keen interest among Christians of all denominations. Some consider it arbitrary. It is necessary to be arbitrary when there is question of truth or right principles. A professor of mathematics must be arbitrary with regard to the mathematic tables. He knows that twice five are ten, and he can not compromise on that. A judge on the bench must be arbitrary. His ruling must be in accordance with the law. Where there is question of truth its spokesman is not free to make concessions or compromises. Christ Himself, the most gentle person that this world has known, was also the most arbitrary when there was question of His teaching. Only they compromise who are not certain of their position. If a man has a clear title to a piece of property he will not compromise with a claimant.

"But," it may be objected, "the very point at issue is the Pope's possession of the truth. He speaks as if he alone were right and everyone differing with him wrong. It is the pretension that His Church alone teaches the truth of Christ that causes resentment against him and the Church which he represents." Let us look into this matter and see if this objection have weight.

Christians believe that Christ is God; that He taught certain definite truths; that He established a Church to perpetuate His ministry; and that He promised to abide with this Church forever. He so intimately identified Himself with the Church which He founded that He said of her: "He that heareth you, heareth Me." (Lk. x. 16.) Christ did not write a book, nor did He inscribe His teaching in letters across the sky. Yet He came to impart the truth not only to the people of His day but to all mankind to the end of the world. His teaching is not in the air nor carved on stone. Yet if it was to be for all time it had to be deposited somewhere for safeguarding and transmission.

Christ did not write the Gospels. The Gospels did not make the Church. The Church of Christ was founded and flourishing before a line of the Gospels was written. The Church of Christ would be just what she is if a line of the Gospels had never been written. It was the Church that gave us the Gospels. She had all the truths of the Gospels, and much more, before the evangelists committed them to writing. Christ said in founding His Church: "All power is given to Me in heaven and on earth. . . . As the Father hath sent Me, I also send you. . . . Go ye therefore and teach all nations whatsoever I have commanded you: and behold I am with you all days, even to the consummation of the world." (Mt. xxviii. 18-20.) (Jn. xx. 21.) Christ therefore established a teaching Church and promised to abide with her always. The Church established by Christ is somewhere in the world to-day and has been from the beginning of Christianity. It is clear that the Church of Christ—whichever it be—can not teach error.

The question resolves itself to this, therefore: Which of the claimants is the Church of Christ? To go into this question historically would take more time than you or I have. Suffice it to say that until the sixteenth century Western Christendom knew but one Church which originated with Christ and that was the Catholic Church. In the sixteenth century, however, there arose some who contended that this Church had fallen into error, that she was teaching false doctrine. Pardon me if I speak plainly. On the one hand was Christ, Who declared that His Church would never teach false doctrine. On the other hand were those who charged her with teaching most blasphemous falsehood. Either Christ was false in His promise, or these men were false in their charges. If these men were right, Christ failed in His promise and consequently the foundation of Christianity crumbled, for Christ can not be God if He failed to keep His guarantee.

They who reject Christianity altogether because they deny the divinity of Christ are consistent. But they who call themselves Christians and yet hold that Christ's guaranteed Church failed, are not consistent for they profess belief in a discredited Christianity. If the one Church in the world which was admittedly the Church of Christ, failed to preserve and teach the truth, as they contend who withdrew from her in the sixteenth century, it was an admission on their part that Christianity had failed and they should have rejected it altogether. For my part, I must say that I would renounce Christianity this minute if I could believe that the Church established by Christ could ever teach error.

The position of Catholics, therefore, and of

the Pope is this: they firmly believe—and are willing to die for their belief—that the Catholic Church is the Church established by Jesus Christ and guaranteed by His divine promise to teach only truth in matters of faith and morals. This being so, the Pope—who is the visible head and spokesman of the Church of which Christ is the Invisible Head—can not, without betraying his trust, make any concession with regard to the body of truths which Christ has committed to His Church.

Those of various Christian denominations who believe that their Church is the Church of Christ, may justify themselves subjectively; but when we realize that truth is unchangeable, and observe, nevertheless, how the various denominations continually change their confession of faith we must admit that objectively their creeds can not be those of Him Who said: "I will ask the Father, and He shall give you another Paraclete, that He may abide with you forever—the Spirit of Truth." (Jn. xiv. 16.)

Recently a distinguished prelate of an Evangelical Church renounced his high office and became a Catholic layman. When asked by his former religionists why he had left the Church which had so honored him, he replied, referring to his former Church: "Authority is a farce in our Church, and Christ's Church can not be one whose authority is not respected. Our prelates are ordinarily afraid to exercise their supposed authority, knowing that it will not be respected." These words are not mine, but those of a former distinguished prelate of another Church.

The Pope, being objectively as well as subjectively certain that He speaks for the true Church of Christ was not arrogant, but loyal to Christ in stating that although he was willing to give his life for the unity of Christian Churches he could not betray his sacred trust for even such a desirable attainment as the unity of Christendom. Only the spokesman of a divine religion could speak out with the firmness of the Pope, in spite of all the inducements and threats made to have him compromise. In this he manifests the efficacy of the words of Christ, Who said to Peter the first Pope: "I have prayed for thee, that thy faith fail not: and thou, being once converted confirm thy brethren." (Lk. xxii. 32.)

CHAPTER V

RELIGION AND SCIENCE

GOD is the Author of Nature and also the Author of Revelation. God is Truth itself. He speaks by nature's voice as well as by the voice of Revelation. Science in the meaning in which it is ordinarily used has to do with the study of natural phenomena. It seeks to explain nature and her laws. There are some who affirm that science and Revelation are in conflict. They contend that the findings of science contradict the Christian religion. Since God is the Author of Nature and also of the Christian religion there can be no real contradiction between science and Christianity. Where there is apparent contradiction it is because either Christianity or science is falsely represented.

Scientist and *science* are two very different terms. A scientist may be wrong but science is never wrong. Science is the truth about nature. A scientist is a person striving after the truth about nature. Scientists sometimes think they have learned the truth about nature only to find subsequently that they were mistaken.

Scientists may be opposed to religion but science never. Let me give you an illustration:

A short time ago a great discovery was announced by some scientists. They found what they declared to be a part of the skull of the missing link—a species between man and monkey—and affirmed that it proved the descent of man from the monkey. Evolutionists throughout the world hailed the discovery with keen satisfaction. The newspapers reported the discovery in large headlines. Those who were looking for confirmation of the man-monkey theory convinced themselves that now at last man's monkey ancestry was a proven fact. On closer scientific examination, however, it developed that the supposed part of the skull of a man-monkey was an elephant's kneecap. In this case some scientists were wrong, not science itself.

Within the past decade there was found in a Western deposit what scientists of repute declared to be the tooth of a creature that was intermediary between monkey and man. This tooth was presented to the learned world as positive proof that man's ancestry was from the ape family. Some of the most distinguished evolutionists of the country accepted the tooth as that of a species between man and monkey. Among others who were so convinced was the curator of a Museum of Natural History. This tooth attracted wide attention, and was regarded as such a precious find and such a convincing proof of the man-monkey theory that it was guarded with the precautions which are employed for the safety of crown-jewels. After several years of exploitation, however, upon examination by scientists whose wish was not father to the thought, it was found that "the million dollar specimen" was nothing but a pig's tooth. In this case, again, it was not science that was wrong, but some scientists, including some very dogmatic scientists.

Some so-called scientists find fault with what they term the dogmatism of Christianity. But religion never dogmatized as do some so-called scientists. True scientists are slow to draw conclusions. Not so the superficial scientists.

At times, however, the best scientists are wrong. Take, for instance, the matter of spontaneous generation. Until Pasteur proved the fallacy of spontaneous generation it was accepted as an established fact by scientists. Before Harvey discovered the circulation of the blood in 1628, scientists were mistaken as to the function of the heart and the flow of the blood. Other instances might be cited where scientists were in error, but not science. What we have stated is sufficient to show that scientists may be opposed to a thing, without science's being opposed to it.

Not so long ago Darwinism was taken for granted as an established scientific fact. Those who did not accept it were considered bigoted or ignorant or retrograde. To-day there is hardly a first-class scientist who believes in Darwinism as proclaimed and accepted a half century ago. This is a broad statement and demands corroboration, which I proceed to give.

In the Journal of the Linnean Society, Vol. XIX, we read as follows: "At present it would be impossible to find any working naturalist who supposes that survival of the fittest is competent to explain all the phenomena of species formation." Yet we can remember when the "survival of the fittest" was a scientific dogma.

Professor Vines, in his presidential address to the Linnean Society, says: "It is established that natural selection, though it may have perpetuated species, can not have originated any." Yet "natural selection" was the Darwinian gospel only a few years ago.

Bateson, then President of the British Association of Scientists, probably the most learned scientific body of the world, stated in his address to the society, 1914, that Darwinism was dead.

Here are his words: "Darwin speaks no more with philosophic authority. We read his scheme of evolution as we would those of Lucretius or Lamarck." Darwinism is not present-day evolution, nevertheless it was the evolution of its day, and is now condemned by evolutionists themselves.

Virchow, founder of cellular pathology, in his address to the Twentieth Century Congress of the German Anthropological Association, declares: "Natural science, so long as it remains science, works only with really existing objects. A hypothesis may be discussed, but its significance can be established only by producing actual proofs in its favor, either by experiment or direct observation. This, Darwinism has not succeeded in doing. In vain have its adherents sought for connecting links which should connect man with the monkey."

Thus speaks Virchow, one of the greatest authorities on anthropology that the world has known. Yet in magazines and on lecture platforms and in some of our school text-books this discarded man-monkey theory is proclaimed a fact, and our people are fed on it, and relish it. No wonder that so many of the present generation—believing that they are only high-grade animals—live by monkey standards. Companionate marriage, petting parties, jungle dances, naked exhibitions, proclaim only too distinctly why certain people readily believe in the man-monkey fable.

Professor Fleischman, says: "The Darwinian theory of descent has not a single fact to confirm it in the realm of nature. It is not the result of scientific research, but purely the product of the imagination." (Die Darwinische Theorie.) If the Catholic Church had made that pronouncement on the man-monkey theory she would have been considered biased or ignorant.

The biologist Ranke concludes his researches on the descent of man as follows: "The only statement consistent with her dignity that science can make is to say that she knows nothing about the origin of man." (Modern Biology, p. 480.)

Notwithstanding this scientific judgment, Catholics are supposed to give up their religion for the hollow statements of pseudo-scientists. We are asked to give up the religion divinely founded by Jesus Christ, for a pig's tooth or an elephant's kneecap. The Church, founded by Jesus Christ, the Son of God, and whose doctrine has not changed in twenty centuries and never will change, is nevertheless asked to surrender to the unsupported theories of superficial scientists.

It is positively criminal to mislead our people, and especially our children, as is done in a Museum of Natural History where man's presumed evolution from the ape is represented in the various stages of the process.

Science is not opposed to Revelation; but pseudo-science is opposed to Revelation and to common sense and to historic facts. Whenever it is said that there is conflict between religion and science it is between false science and true religion, or between true science and false religion. Between true science and the true religion there can be no conflict.

Hence, because the Catholic Church is as true as God she welcomes true science, and has always been the patroness of science. She founded the Universities of Oxford and Cambridge which are now the proud boast of England. Pasteur, the greatest scientist of modern times, was a devout Catholic. He found no conflict between religion and science. Fabre, the world's most distinguished entomologist, was a sincere Catholic, whose Faith was so dear to him that he said: "You might as well try to take the skin from my body as to take away my Faith." He stated moreover that the more he knew of science the more he valued his Faith.

There may be contradictions between science

and some of the ever-changing man-made religions which label themselves Christian; but between true science and the Catholic Church there can never be real opposition, for God can not speak one way by His Church and another way by Creation.

Time is the test of truth. Time has always justified Catholic truth. As it was said of Christ, so it is said now by some opponents of His Church "can any good come out of Nazareth?" Christ, *the Way, the Truth,* and *the Life,* came out of Nazareth. So to-day is the Church of Christ the Light of the World. This is not arrogance, but faith in Him Who said: "He who followeth Me, walketh not in darkness." (Jn. vii. 12.) The Church of Christ is the Christian compass which securely directs mankind to everlasting life.

CHAPTER VI

RELIGION AND AUTHORITY

ON account of the deep and widespread interest in the recent Encyclical of the Holy Father on Church Unity, it is advisable to inform those of all creeds that in speaking so authoritatively the Pope does not do so from arrogance but from the very nature of the religion of which Christ is the Invisible Head and of which the Pope is the Living Voice. In order that the public may be rightly informed on the pronouncement of the Pope, I shall speak on the nature of the authority of the Church of Christ.

Every government must have authority or cease to function. A government that can not enforce its laws is no longer a government. *To govern* means *to control* or *to direct.* When a government can not effectually control or direct its subjects it has no reason for existence. Rather it is an evil, because a government, powerless to win respect for, and obedience to its authority encourages anarchy. A business concern, without an authoritative head, would soon meet with failure. An army deprived of a central source of authority would degenerate into a mob. Even a family must respect the authority of its head if it is to remain a real family. All this is the veriest platitude. However a platitude is sometimes necessary to bring home a very commonplace but overlooked truth.

There is an idea abroad now that authority implies servitude or inferiority. Nothing is further from the truth. Authority implies order, welfare, achievement. People in authority are under authority as much as those over whom they rule. No matter what may be a person's position in life it does not free him from authority. In fact, the higher one's position, the higher one's responsibility. There is really no one under more authority than a monarch. It is true he may make laws or help to make them, and he may have great latitude of conduct, but all the while he is ruled and governed by a code of custom and of popular exactions which bind him much more than his subjects are bound by the general laws. The higher a person is in authority the less he has of freedom.

The story is told of Roosevelt, that, when he was President of the United States, he was accustomed occasionally to cross over the Potomac into Virginia on a hunting trip. On one occasion he picked up a colored lad in Alexandria to carry his game-bag. The boy did not know who the man was. It happened to be a good day for hunting, and the President made some very remarkable shots. Finally he sighted a bird on the wing at a great distance, and flying at top speed. He raised his gun and while doing so the lad ejaculated: "Mister, you sure ain't going to try to get that one!" Before he finished the sentence Roosevelt had fired and the bird was beginning to fall earthward.

"Gee!" exclaimed the boy, "you certainly am a good shot." With eyes as big as saucers he added: "Mister, may I ask your name?" To which the President replied: "My name is Roosevelt."

For a moment the boy was stunned, then he said slowly: "You ain't the Mister Roosevelt what's President of these here United States, be you?"

The President replied: "Yes, my boy, I think I am that gentleman."

There was a brief pause, and then the lad looking up in admiration gave a low whistle and said: "Gee you are the only man in the country what ain't got a boss!"

"Son," rejoined the President, "I am the only man in the country who has a million bosses."

Roosevelt was right. Position and power make one answerable for the right use of one's authority.

In the days of absolute monarchy a ruler could place himself more or less outside and above the law. Such monarchs were known as tyrants and were hated by their subjects. Moreover, they fell into a slavery of fear which was worse than subjection to authority.

It is all very well to speak about liberty and independence. But the matter of fact is that no rational being can be his own master if he is to live in human society. In proportion as others respect our liberty we must respect theirs. This at once constitutes a restriction, and restrictions multiply with rights and liberties. For example citizens have a right to protection in the streets. This right imposes on drivers of vehicles the law regulating speed. People have a right to be safeguarded from contagious disease. This imposes health laws on the public and other restrictions, such as quarantine and various kinds of inspection.

In proportion as a government has its rightful authority respected, will the people be happier and better and more truly free. Where authority is not respected we have license not liberty, as witness those countries where lawlessness and brigandage prevail. Only those prate about being free and independent who know nothing about freedom and independence. Nothing makes for the peace and welfare of a community as do law and order. No society can long exist without unified direction either directly or indirectly. In fact, between the two evils of absolutism and license, absolutism is preferable. Mexico under Diaz and under the régimes since is proof. An army under a martinet is better off than an army under a weakling head who is afraid or unable to exercise authority. Any temporary advantage acquired by license exacts in the end a heavy toll.

Authority, therefore, does not imply servitude nor inferiority nor any undue restriction of freedom. We say this because there are some people to-day who condemn the Catholic Church because she is authoritative. Instead of being an objection to the Catholic Church *authority* is an argument for her.

Recently a professor of one of our nationally known universities became a convert to Catholicism. On being asked why he took such a step, he replied that it was because the Catholic Church was the only one that spoke and acted with real authority. His questioner said to this: "Why, you have surrendered your will and judgment to an organization." To which the professor replied: "Not to an organization, but to God." To this his objector said: "Why could you not submit your will and judgment to God in our Church?" "Because," said the professor, "God speaks with authority, and the only Church in the world that so speaks is the Roman Catholic Church."

The very thing that repels unthinking people from the Catholic Church attracts thinkers to her. Since religion is a bond between the Creator and creature it should be evident that unless the bond really brings contact it serves no purpose. A religion which does not bind to what is certain and authoritative does not bind to God, Who is certainty itself, and authority personified. On reflection this must be evident. Religion to have a sanction must have divinity back of it. Divinity is authoritative and true. Without sanction, religion is only a human code not binding in conscience and not capable of influencing mankind effectively. Hence a divine religion must be authoritative and true.

One of the greatest credentials of the Catholic Church is her authority and her certainty. Man wants to know for certain what he must do, and to be told in no hesitating manner to do it. People cheerfully carry out orders which are given with due command, and which are surely obligatory. The Catholic realizes that in matters of faith and morals the Church commands in the name and with the authority of Christ. This gives Catholics that comfort and peace in the practice of their religion which is in itself part of the reward promised by Christ for following Him. A little consideration will show that *authoritative* religion is the only one worthy of the name.

CHAPTER VII

RELIGION AND THE MODERN MIND

WE are living in a practical age. Religion—as well as government, business and society—is put to the working test. For nearly twenty centuries the Church of God has stood the test of time and the white light of common sense. In fact, the stronger the light thrown on her the more she shows divine. The purpose of these talks is to view the teaching of the Church through the eyes of common sense.

The true religion must be a sensible religion. God gave us our common sense, and any religion which is opposed to common sense can not be His. The Creator gave us our nature. A divine religion must answer to the proper needs of human nature. I say *proper needs,* not the needs resulting from passion or vice.

Recently I was in conversation with a gentleman who had traveled very extensively and who was then a representative of the United States at a foreign court. He was not a Catholic. Perceiving that he was a close observer of men and affairs, I asked him if he had ever formed an opinion of the Catholic Church. He answered immediately: "Why yes. I have been particularly impressed by the moderation of the Catholic Church. Whenever we diplomats discuss affairs which directly or indirectly concern religious questions we invariably remark the moderation which your Church displays."

His statement keenly interested me, and moved me to ask further in what, particularly, he had noticed this moderation. To my surprise he said: "In mostly all practical matters I have observed that your Church holds the common sense position. Take, for instance, the observance of Sunday. Your Church has always avoided the extremes of laxity and severity. It is the same also with regard to amusements, such as card-playing, dancing and various other forms of entertainment. She holds a middle course, regulating—not abolishing—these diversions. The attitude of your Church towards temperance is another case in point. She does not condemn the use of liquor but only its abuse. I might go on and enumerate other matters which illustrate my meaning but you know them," said he, "even better than I." We talked together for several hours, discussing such topics as war, divorce, education, capital and labor, science, art, and politics; towards all of which he noted that the attitude of the Catholic Church was that of moderation.

Christ was the best example of moderation that this world has known. Consider how He restrained the excessive zeal of His apostles when they wished the chastisement of heaven to fall on those who would not receive Him: "He rebuked them, saying: You know not of what spirit you are. The Son of Man came not to destroy souls, but to save." (Lk. ix. 55, 56.)

No one hated sin so much as did Christ, yet no one ever showed greater kindness to a repentant sinner than He. Magdalene, whom the supposedly righteous people of Jerusalem scorned, was not only forgiven by Him but made the companion of His blessed Mother. One of the few who stood at the foot of the cross with Mary, His Mother, was Mary Magdalene. Christ willingly died to atone for sin, nevertheless towards the repentant sinner He was full of tenderest mercy.

Everything in life is subject to abuse. If we abolish whatever was abused there is nothing in use among mankind—no matter how good or serviceable—that would not have to be abolished. It would be possible to prevent all automobile accidents by doing away with automobiles. But that would be to deprive of their use all those who exercise common sense and restraint with regard to them. It would be penalizing right users for the wrong-doing of those who abused a distinctly good and serviceable thing.

It is in avoiding extremes which concern mankind that the Church has been conspicuous from the beginning. This does not mean that the Church is a weak institution, afraid to take a stand against corruption or abuse. On the contrary she has shown herself throughout the ages the firmest and most courageous champion of right. She stood up bravely before emperors and multitudes whenever it was necessary to defend virtue or truth. It was she who rebuked the great Theodosius for his cruelty, and condemned Henry VIII for his adultery. She lost the English nation rather than compromise on the permanence of the marriage bond. To-day when nearly every creed makes concessions which undermine matrimony, she upholds marriage as Christ instituted it. And she does this in face of opposition from without and of human frailty from within her fold.

Moderation is by no means weakness. In point of fact moderation is an indication of strength. They who go to extremes in any cause have either a poor cause or lack the strength rightly to uphold a good cause. Christ, the most moderate person that this world has known, was also the firmest. In matters of right and wrong He was inflexible. But in the application of principle to conduct He showed Himself broad, wise and most humane. When the Pharisees complained that His disciples did not observe certain restrictions of the Sabbath, He defended them, proclaiming that the Sabbath was made for man, not man for the Sabbath.

Again, when He was accused of consorting with sinners He declared that not those who were well needed the physician but those who were ill. No one condemned sin more than Christ, yet when the holier-than-thou accusers brought to Him a woman taken in sin He bade those among them who were guiltless to cast the first stone at her. Not that he condoned vice, but that He condemned hypocrisy. Moreover He would teach these false leaders that justice must be tempered with mercy. His Church does likewise. A priest of His Church would give his life to prevent sin, and would also give his life to reclaim a sinner. Christ called Himself the Good Shepherd. Like a shepherd He not only cared for the sheep that were safe but went after those that had strayed. In His Church there is a religious order of noble women who consecrate their lives to the work of bringing back into the Fold unfortunate ones who have strayed or fallen by the wayside. The Order of The Good Shepherd is a living testimony that the spirit of Christ animates the Catholic Church. In point of fact the spirit of Christ characterizes His Church throughout. If it did not she would not be the true Church.

Although Christ was so tender and merciful He nevertheless declared that following Him might at times be very painful even causing the loss of one's life. But He added: "He that shall lose his life for My sake, shall find it." It is so with His Church. Some doctrines of Christ may at times require great sacrifices for their observance. The Church does not for this reason modify His teaching but insists that pain or loss must be endured for what is right and true. Some churches abolish a doctrine if it entails hardship or discomfort, as if Christ came to teach only what was acceptable to man. But He came to teach the truth—the way to everlasting life; and if that way should be at times steep and rough it must be trod even if it leave bloody footprints.

It is the marvelous combination of moderation and firmness that so much impresses the student of Christ and of Christ's Church. Moderation may easily degenerate into laxity, and firmness into cruelty. But Christ was neither lax nor cruel. It is so with His Church. Abuses there have been in the Church; but no one deplored them more than she herself. Christ's Church has never taught a lax doctrine, nor, on the other hand, gone to extremes in inculcating morality. This does not mean that she has been narrow or timid, but that she has displayed that moderation and common sense which must characterize a religion that is true and divine.

It may seem to some that the history of the early Church, which records the martyrdom of so many of her children, would indicate that she was a cruel Mother to demand loyalty at the cost of such extreme suffering. But extreme measures do not always imply going to extremes. At times extreme measures are the wisest and the only means of action. To throw a cargo overboard to save the ship is an extreme measure, but it is not going to extremes. For what avails the cargo if the ship with all aboard go down? Man's mortal life is precious, but not so precious as to lose immortal life to retain it. Christ advocated extreme measures only in extreme issues. Where this life and eternal life come in conflict there is no question which must be sacrificed. Hence Christ said: "What exchange shall a man give for his soul?" (Mt. xvi. 26.)

On examination, therefore, it appears that even such an extreme measure as martyrdom is moderation in the true meaning of the term, since it is the employment of common sense in an issue in which more is involved than the whole world. The burning of Moscow was an extreme measure, but it was not going to extremes since the destruction of that one city was the saving of a nation.

Religion has to do with man's temporal and eternal well-being. Often there is no conflict between the two. But at times there may be; and in such cases there can be no question which is preferable, if one is to be directed by common sense. "For what shall it profit a man, if he gain the whole world, and suffer the loss of his soul?" (Mk. viii. 36.) A common-sense merchant looks not merely to the profit of the moment, but to future prosperity and stability. The Church of Christ bids her children to use like common sense in striving for eternal welfare.

CHAPTER VIII

SEX MATTERS

THE dominant passion of mankind is that which relates to sex. The Author of Nature implanted the sex instinct in man in order to assure the perpetuation of the human race. Like every human instinct the sex impulse must be under the control of reason. Some people assert that since the sex impulse is natural it should be given free rein. They say: "Why are our tendencies given us if not to follow?"

The drunkard follows his tendencies, and it lowers him to the level of the beast. The dope-fiend follows his tendencies, and it makes him a human wreck. The thief follows his tendencies, and it puts him behind prison bars. The greatest fallacy ever uttered is that we should follow, rather than control, our impulses. Giving way to anger makes a man temporarily insane. Indulging the appetite for food without restraint makes dyspeptics and invalids. No! Man was given reason to rule his animal tendencies, and every time that reason gives way to passion, nature exacts a heavy toll. Our hospitals, prisons, and insane asylums are filled with the victims of uncontrolled tendencies and passions.

In no career of life may we be controlled by our feelings. The merchant must attend to business although he may feel a strong desire for rest or entertainment. The professional man must be affable when his inclinations prompt him to be indignant or sharp. No one can remain in good society unless he control his impulses in conformity with the social code.

Sex impulse, above all, requires rational control or it will hurl a man over a precipice. There are more disasters, diseases, tragedies and wrecks from uncontrolled sex impulses than from any other one cause. If sex impulse be properly controlled it means that man's life generally will be rightly regulated. For control of the dominant passion indicates control of the lesser ones. Passion controlled is like a spirited horse under firm rein. But passion uncontrolled is like a fiery steed under loose rein. Restraint is the law of life. The successful athlete must restrain himself in many ways. The successful statesman must restrain his sentiments. The successful leader of men must restrain his likes and dislikes.

In every normal person there is a conflict between rational and animal nature. We approve of what is good but find ourselves drawn to evil. So great a saint as the Apostle Paul found this conflict in himself between soul and body. Chesterton has said that if Revelation did not teach the fact of original sin man would have to invent some such doctrine to explain the conflict in human nature.

Man is the only being in which there is internal conflict. Animals have external foes. Man's greatest foe is within. His greatest battles are with himself. He must either master his passions or become their slave. There is no slavery like that forged by evil habits, as witness the drug-addict or the victim of sex offenses. It is doubtless an effort at times to control our passions, but the consequence of not controlling them is more painful than the effort to control. An act repeated generates a tendency. A tendency unchecked forms a habit. A habit forges the chains of slavery. There is no misery on earth comparable to that of the victim of uncontrolled sex impulse.

It is often asked why the Catholic Church lays such stress on purity of morals. It is because, with the wisdom of God, she knows that nothing makes for personal and social welfare so much as purity of mind and body. This calls for self-mastery or self-denial. Christ proclaimed: "If any man will be my disciple let him deny himself." (Lk. ix. 23.) Self-denial is the fundamental principle of the Christian life. Self-control in sex matters is the key to peace, welfare and salvation. Many crimes are connected, either directly or indirectly, with sex offenses. Lying, theft, jealousy, revenge, murder, are often directly or indirectly associated with sex sins. In brief, unless man control sex, sex will control him; and the sex-controlled man is the most miserable slave on earth.

We should not be surprised, therefore, that the Church of God so carefully directs and safeguards her children with regard to sex and all that it implies. We should rather expect a divine religion to teach mankind the most effective way of controlling the dominant passion, and making it serve the beneficial and salutary purpose which the Author of Nature intends.

We hear a great deal at present about psychology and mental suggestion. Because the Church of Christ is divine she knows the soul of man without the science of psychology. She is taught of God and guided by the Holy Spirit.

Psychology affirms that mental suggestion has a strong, sometimes an overpowering, influence on bodily action. The Church of Christ, as a true psychologist, guards her children against mental suggestion relative to sex matters. She forbids immoral thoughts and dangerous occasions of sin. She knows that immoral thoughts ordinarily beget immoral deeds. In this she is voicing the teaching of Christ Who said: "For from within out of the heart of men proceed evil thoughts, adulteries, fornications, murders." (Mk. vii. 21.)

In matters of sex there is an intimate relation between thought and deed. When therefore the Catholic Church declares that man's thoughts must be clean she is not only proclaiming what Christ explicitly taught but is also prescribing what psychology affirms to be the best possible means of maintaining purity of life. It is almost impossible to harbor lustful thoughts or to frequent dangerous occasions without falling into lustful deeds. Dangerous occasions engender bad thoughts. Bad thoughts tend to bad deeds. The Church therefore in forbidding dangerous occasions and impure thoughts strikes at the very root of sex offenses. Like a wise and skilled physician, she does not limit her prescriptions to symptoms of disease, but seeks their root and applies the remedy there. Christ, the greatest of psychologists, declared: "Blessed are the clean of heart: for they shall see God." (Mt. v. 8.)

It has always been a problem with good people, what policy to pursue with regard to sex instruction. Modesty is the guardian of purity. Modest people are ordinarily pure in thought and deed. Knowledge of evil does not keep people from evil. Those who know most about the evil consequences of impurity frequently become the worst victims of the vice of impurity. Perhaps never before in the history of mankind was there so much sex instruction as at present, and never before were there so many victims of the vice of impurity. Our predecessors got along without all the sex instruction that is now ruining so many under pretext of educating them. The purest and healthiest nations of the world have been those least acquainted with sex knowledge. There is a natural instinct in this matter which dictates reserve. A few words of discreet instruction from the proper persons at the right time is all that is necessary for sexual guidance.

The policy of the Church of Christ has always been to safeguard purity by upholding lofty ideals and virtuous principles. But above all the Catholic Church develops pure generations by having her children realize that impurity is a sin. It is forbidden by Almighty God. That is the great and sufficient reason for avoiding sex offenses.

In order to safeguard persons against smallpox, it is not necessary to familiarize them with the symptoms of the dread disease. The health officers put up a warning sign and people keep away from the scourge. God, the highest authority, labels impurity a sin, and declares that the impure shall not enter the kingdom of heaven. That is more effective against sex offense than all the means devised by man. Moreover in order to help her children to be pure the Church nourishes them with the grace-giving sacraments established by her divine Founder. It is impossible to partake frequently and worthily of the sacraments and become a victim of sex-domination.

Unfortunately many of the youth of to-day are taught that they are but high-grade animals. God has no part in their lives. They are a law unto themselves. We see the result only too clearly and painfully. These misguided ones are repeating the sentiments of the wicked of old as recorded in Scripture: "The time of our life is short . . . come therefore, and let us enjoy the good things that are present . . . let us crown ourselves with roses, before they be withered:

let no meadow escape our riot. . . . Let our strength be the law of justice. . . . These things they thought, and were deceived: for their own wickedness blinded them." (Wisdom ii. 1, 6, 8, 11, 21.) Too late did these victims of vice discover their error. The Bible gives us their words of despair: "We wearied ourselves in the way of iniquity and destruction, and have walked through hard ways, but the way of the Lord we have not known . . . but we are consumed in our wickedness. Such things the sinners said in hell." (Wisdom v. 7.13.14.)

In contrast to those who were a law to themselves defying God's will, is the end of those who reverenced the law of God: "But the just shall live for evermore: and their reward is with the Lord . . . therefore shall they receive a kingdom of glory, and a crown of beauty from the hand of the Lord." (Wisdom v. 16.17.) Let me conclude with the inspiring words and glorious promise of our Divine Saviour: "Blessed are the clean of heart: for they shall see God." (Mt. v. 8.)

CHAPTER IX

MARRIAGE

IT is doubtful if there is anything more vital to human society than marriage. The family is the basis of society, and marriage is the basis of the family. If the marriage bond be loose, both family and society will suffer. If the marriage bond be firm, both family and society will be secure. History attests that wherever and whenever marriage has been regarded lightly by a people disaster has followed.

The home is the heart of the nation. Citizenship and patriotism depend on the character of the home. Men who have good homes and beloved families will serve well and loyally the country which protects them. The home will be right, ordinarily, if the marriage bond be right and respected.

People sometimes ask why the Catholic Church puts so much importance on marriage. It is because Christ has set her the example. Rather it is because she is carrying out His solemn mandate in the matter. The Catholic

Church did not institute Christian marriage. Christian marriage is the institution of Jesus Christ Who elevated it to the dignity of a sacrament. In the design of the Creator marriage was intended as the proper means of perpetuating the human race. Originally, marriage was a perpetual bond between one man and one woman, but human license had eventually weakened it and lowered it from its high estate. Christ restored marriage to its original status, and moreover dignified it by making it a sacred rite of His holy religion.

With regard to Christian marriage the Catholic Church teaches precisely what her divine Founder taught. She is not free to alter the nature of marriage as proclaimed by Jesus Christ. As long as the world lasts the Catholic Church will not change one essential feature of the sacrament of matrimony, regardless of what changes may be advocated or made by others.

Christ proclaimed the nature of the marriage contract but left to His Church the details pertaining to its performance. Whenever the Catholic Church legislates on marriage it is only with regard to the formalities which must be observed in making the contract valid. Once the Christian marriage contract is duly made the Church regards it just as Christ regarded it, and it is not in her power to regard it otherwise. Christ declared that marriage was indissoluble. His Church so declares, and will so declare until the end of time.

When Christ proclaimed marriage indissoluble, He had in mind a valid marriage. Marriage, like any civil contract, may be valid or invalid. If a civil contract be valid the courts will uphold it regardless of consequences. If a civil contract be invalid the courts will not break the contract but will declare that no contract existed. So with regard to marriage. If a marriage be validly performed the Church will uphold it in face of the whole world. But if it be not validly performed the Church will declare it null and void. In doing this she does not break the marriage bond, but proclaims that no bond existed. However we shall consider this aspect of the matter more at length in our talk next week, when we shall consider the subject of divorce.

Marriage may be defined as a legitimate union between man and woman constituting them man and wife. By *legitimate union* is meant a union sanctioned by law, whether the law be racial, civil or ecclesiastical. The term *man and wife* signifies mutual rights of sexual intercourse, life in common, and permanent union.

Sexual intercourse which does not imply life in common and permanence is not marriage but concubinage.

The marriage of an individual person of one sex to an individual person of the other sex is called monogamy. Opposed to monogamy is polygamy, the marriage of one man to several women. Polygamy debases and demoralizes woman. Monogamy is the recognized form of marriage among civilized people. The experience of mankind, the voice of nature and the institution of Jesus Christ proclaim that monogamy—the marriage of one man to one woman—is the proper form of union for man and wife. Every nation that has been Christianized recognizes and upholds monogamous marriage only.

Next in importance to the union of one man with one woman in marriage is the permanency of the union. The nature of marriage is such that temporary union is incompatible with its purpose. We must consider marriage as an institution affecting not this or that individual, but the human race. Also we must keep in mind that there is no law nor institution among mankind that does not cause some individuals pain, loss or hardship of one kind or another. If we abolish a law because of its occasional hardships or abuses, we should have to abolish every law and every institution in the world. Taxes, speed laws, health laws, etc., at times cause great inconvenience and even hardship on individuals, but the welfare of the public at large demands nevertheless that these laws be carried into effect. So with marriage, the good of mankind requires that in spite of incidental hardship the bond be permanent.

By nature man is drawn to associate sexually with woman. Nature's purpose in this union is the perpetuation of the human race. The natural and ordinary result of marriage is offspring. In exceptional cases children may not be the outcome of sex relationship, but they are the normal and ordinary consequence. Children have the natural right to the care, protection and love of father and mother. Unless marriage be permanent children are deprived of this natural right.

If death remove either parent that is the affair of Providence. The Creator has the right to rule the world as He sees fit, and the wisdom to dispose of His creatures for their ultimate welfare. God is the Author of Nature, man is His subject and bound by nature's laws. Hence for man to deprive his children of what nature entitles them to, is the violation of nature's ordinance.

A child by the devotion and sacrifice of either father or mother alone, may be reared satisfactorily, but it is ordinarily exceptional, and always there is left a rancor in the heart of the child who is deprived of either father or mother otherwise than by the hand of death.

Besides the children, the mother must be considered. A mother is not ordinarily independent and free to live her own life. Motherhood has made her responsible for those to whom she has given birth. By marriage she gave her maidenhood to her husband. That can never be restored to her. In giving that she gave what is most precious to woman. In return the man engaged to be her support and protector. Motherhood and wifehood demand permanence of the marriage bond. Civil law recognizes this indirectly, since it obliges man to supply by alimony what is renounced by divorce when for just cause the courts grant the woman a decree of separation.

No man, regarding marriage disinterestedly, would consider it otherwise than permanent. No normal man contracts marriage except with the intention of forming a lasting union. No man living but feels in his heart that the nature of marriage demands permanency. The status of wife, mother and children cry out for the lasting union of the bond of matrimony.

Marriage is no exception to other states of life. In every department of life we must expect difficulties. For the sake of success in business or a profession people must patiently endure many inconveniences and frequently hardships. The home is the biggest business of life. It is worth while exercising restraint and forbearance for the sake of the family just as much and even more than for success in business. The Catholic Church recognizes all the difficulties of married life, and has provided for them by suitable remedies, but not by absolute divorce with the right to re-marry.

Divorce, with right to re-marry, has done more to break up families than all the difficulties and differences that occur in family life. Man is fickle. When he pledges his troth to be faithful to the maiden he takes in marriage he means it. But the heart of man is restless. He seeks novelty. A new face captivates him. Infatuated by a new love he not only loses his love for her to whom he pledged it, but begins to hate her because she is an obstacle to his new attraction. If there were no possibility of a new union he would dismiss from his thoughts the object of his temptation. But with the hope of a new union he seeks to break the old. He creates a condition of incompatibility which eventually leads to the severance of the marriage tie, and then hastens to form a new alliance. Little difficulties and misunderstandings which would vanish or be overcome by patience, if marriage held until death, assume larger and larger proportions where there is prospect of a new union.

For sixteen centuries there was no such thing as divorce in Christendom, and during that period people, although they had their trials then as now, lived contentedly. Single life has its difficulties as well as married life. The only way to avoid difficulties is to cease to be mortal. Every career of life has its misunderstandings and hardships and suffering. Marriage is no exception. Married life offers no immunity from the cares, responsibilities and misunderstandings of life.

Divorce does not remedy marriage ills but aggravates and multiplies them. When a man divorces his wife and marries another he persuades himself that he has found an angel and that his new life will be a path of roses. But before long he finds the thorns as before. Divorce leads to divorce. Many people live more miserably with their second mate than with their first; and yet more miserably with the third.

For Catholics the matter is settled once for all by Him Who made man. God, the Author of

Nature and the Ruler of the World, has proclaimed that marriage is indissoluble. The Catholic Church is the Voice of God in the world. "He that heareth you, heareth Me." (Lk. x. 16.) Hence until the end of time the Catholic Church will echo the words of her divine Founder:

> "From the beginning of the creation, God made them male and female. For this cause a man shall leave his father and mother; and shall cleave to his wife. And they two shall be in one flesh. Therefore now they are not two, but one flesh. What therefore God hath joined together, let not man put asunder. . . . Whosoever shall put away his wife and marry another, committeth adultery against her. And if the wife shall put away her husband, and be married to another, she committeth adultery." (Mk. x. 6-12.)

This is the teaching of Jesus Christ. It is also the teaching of the Church of Christ, and moreover will be her teaching on marriage to the end of time.

CHAPTER X

DIVORCE

RECENTLY a gentleman said to me: "Why is it that your Church, being so strict about divorce, is not stricter about people getting married?" I told him that he would never ask that question if he had ever tried to get married to a Catholic. I then showed him that the Church takes such precautions with marriage that some criticize her for making it too difficult. She takes all this care, and makes her children take it, because marriage is the most consequential contract a human being can make. However, in spite of all her pains and precaution, people do at times make unfortunate marriages.

Most marriage trouble in our day comes about from hasty marriages. Moreover, many of the young people, especially in cities, are altogether unqualified for the duties and exigencies of married life. As young women and young men pass you on the street, and you notice their frivolousness and license you wonder what sort of parents they can become. Young women are almost disguised by artificial devices to beautify themselves; and young men seem to disregard all the proprieties in their association with them. These are the young folks who are to become husband and wife, father and mother. Is it any wonder that in so many cases marriage, after the first few months, settles down to a condition of mere tolerance? Love seems to have departed. Rather it was really never there. It was just sex attraction of the animal sort, which is fickle and selfish. Hence, after marriage, when familiarity discloses the artifices of courtship, and each knows the other for what she or he is, misunderstandings begin.

Incompatibility is a modern matrimonial ailment, due to the fact that it may open the door to a new alliance. When courting, and up to the marriage day, both parties were very compatible. It is true that in the intimate nature of married life, one's defects stand out in a particularly annoying manner. But married life, just as every other career of life, calls for patience and self-restraint.

If, however, in spite of everything, the marriage situation becomes intolerable, as it does sometimes, the Church advises separation rather than to live in sin, for sin it is to live in animosity and at cross-purposes. But separation is advisable only as the very last resort, and with every precaution for the well-being of the children. But although the Church permits separation in extreme cases she never sanctions divorce with right to re-marry.

Until the Protestant Reformation there was no such thing as divorce in Christendom. Luther granted the first divorce to a prince who supported his innovation. Henry VIII in effect granted himself a divorce, in order to marry his wife's maid. Gradually a new doctrine of divorce crept in by interpreting Christ's words permitting separation to mean divorce with right to re-marry. But Christ Himself plainly declared that although separation was lawful under certain circumstances divorce with right to re-marry was never lawful. Here are His words: "Every one that putteth away his wife, and marrieth another, committeth adultery: and he that marrieth her that is put away from her husband, committeth adultery." (Lk. xvi. 18.) It would be impossible to word legislation more unequivocally than that.

.It is a matter of gratification to Catholics to observe that many who are not of the Catholic Faith are beginning to recognize that her position on marriage and divorce is the only right one. Recently a Protestant organization has been formed in order to stem the tide of evil resulting from the moral cancer of divorce. The New York Times, July 6th, 1925, published the following news item:

"The Sanctity of Marriage Association launched a movement yesterday to bar absolutely the marriage of divorced persons in the Protestant Episcopal Church. The Sanctity of Marriage Association is headed by the Rev. Dr. Milo H. Gates, vicar of the Chapel of the Intercession, Trinity Parish; and its Executive Committee includes, among others, Bishop William T. Manning, Bishop Frederick Burgess of Long Island and Bishop Paul Matthews of New Jersey.

"The proposed law is:

"No minister, knowingly after due inquiry, shall solemnize the marriage of any person who has been or is the husband or the wife of any person living from whom he or she has been divorced for any cause arising after marriage. Nor shall it be lawful for any member of this Church to enter upon a marriage when either of the contracting parties is the husband or the wife of any other person then living from whom he or she has been divorced for any cause arising after marriage.

"The association gives the following reasons why in its judgment the one 'exception' should be repealed:

"Because nowhere in the New Testament is there a single word in support of re-marriage of either party after 'putting away' during the lifetime of the other.

"Because nowhere either in the Old or the New Testament is there any assumption, much less assertion, of the modern theory that adultery, or any other sin, *ipso facto,* dissolves a marriage, which is not a mere contract but a state or condition.

"Because nowhere in the history of the first three centuries, when the Church was suffering persecution and was free from all entanglements with the State, can there be found a single author who interprets the exceptive clauses of St. Matthew about 'putting away' as reason for re-marriage during the life of the other party.

"Because nowhere since the fourth century, in the whole Western Church, down to the year 1868 was there any canonical allowance for the re-marriage of the so-called 'innocent party.'

"Because, in accordance with our Lord's pragmatic test, 'by their fruits ye shall know them,' the census reports for the United States, with their forty-eight codes and fifty-two causes for sundering the bond, show the most rapid increase of divorces of any country, pagan or Christian, in the world."

It is a matter of experience that some Catholics who have been married have had the marriage set aside and have re-married. How explain this in view of the Catholic doctrine of the indissolubility of marriage? To understand this we need to know just what constitutes a marriage. It may be said at the outset that among Christians no consummated valid marriage has ever been annulled, and never can be annulled.

Christ recalled and declared the nature of marriage, but left to His Church the regulation of everything else pertaining to it. The Church then decrees how this marriage contract is to be executed. If one makes a civil contract, and it is not done legally, it is null and void before the law. The Church decrees beforehand how the marriage contract must be made, and that only persons who are marriageable may become parties to the contract. She states beforehand the form of the marriage ceremony, and the class of people who are marriageable, and declares solemnly that any contract in violation of these decrees is not a valid marriage.

This power of legislating on the formalities of the marriage ceremony was given to the Church by Christ Himself: "Whatsoever you shall bind on earth, shall be bound also in heaven." (Mt. xviii. 18.)

Whenever, therefore, you hear of Catholics having their marriage set aside and re-marrying, you will know that there was, in the case in question, no valid previous marriage. A so-called Catholic divorce, is no divorce at all, but a declaration that there was no marriage from the beginning. Persons who have their marriage set aside may have very good reasons for not letting the public know why it was done. The Church never informs the public except the case be public, and the reasons for the so-called divorce have been made known by the parties to the divorce.

In business contracts, in government contracts, in army enlistment, and in every other civil matter, the parties to a contract are held to it, regardless of hardship or disillusionment. A clerk in a store does not always find things congenial or satisfactory, but nevertheless continues at work. A young man may enlist in the army or navy and find, after he has signed, that his companions or superior officers or the work is not compatible. But he is held to his enlistment nevertheless. The marriage bond is more binding than enlistment.

Before this modern leprosy of divorce became prevalent, people had their difficulties in married life just as they have now. But because divorce was unheard of, they made up their differences and lived on if not happily, at least satisfactorily.

It cannot be said too plainly that marriage does not change one's nature. What one is before marriage that one will be after marriage. For this reason the Church advises her children to proceed carefully in this matter. Nowadays young people rush into marriage without the consideration that they would exercise in buying a house or an automobile. Then they wonder that they are not suited to each other! They are caught by some superficial or artificial attraction, and without knowing the real person at all take a partner for life. They then blame marriage or the Church for what they themselves are responsible.

Christ came not to remove the cross but to help us carry it. Married life has its cross, as single life has. Nothing so unites a family and makes its members so devoted to one another as the mutual bearing of its hardships, and mutual consideration. Married life calls for the exercise of virtue as well as does single life. Divorce proclaims that separation and re-marriage must take the place of the Christian virtues of patience and forbearance. If the history of mankind teaches any lesson unmistakably it is that divorce is the moral cancer of society, of the family, and of the individual. After all, man cannot improve on God.

CHAPTER XI

MARRIAGE AND ANNULMENT

IT is safe to say that the most important natural institution for human welfare is marriage. A nation is vigorous in proportion to the correctness of its family life; and proper family life depends in great part on the character of marriage. Not only the nation as a whole, but its individual members, as well, are affected vitally by the nature of marriage.

People whose home life is satisfactory not only love home but country also. Men and youths whose family life is attractive will defend home and country at all cost. Those whose home is congenial will be concerned for the government which safeguards the home. Thus it is that the home makes patriots; and patriotism is the best defense of country. It is the home that attaches people to country and government. It is home welfare that gives man inspiration to achieve and to endure. It is to make the home ever better that urges man to worthy ambition.

The home accordingly is a most important factor in individual and national life.

It is common sense therefore to take every right means in order to maintain the home in its integrity. A business man makes many personal sacrifices for the success of his business, whatever it may be. The biggest business of life is the family. No matter what success one may have in trade, in society, or in public office, if family life is not right, one has not made a success of life. On the other hand, if one's family life is what it should be, one is able to face the vicissitudes of life in a spirit of buoyancy, which if it does not ensure material success at least affords strength and courage to cope with every obstacle.

The experience of mankind as well as the voice of nature proclaims that monogamy, the marriage of one man to one woman, is the proper form of union for man and wife. It is common sense therefore to uphold monogamy. And this is what the Catholic Church has done from the beginning. Through her teaching and efforts every country which has been Christianized recognizes monogamous marriage only. At times polygamy has been the greatest obstacle to her missionary efforts.

Next in importance to the union of one man

with one woman in marriage, is the permanency of the union. The nature of matrimony is such that temporary union is incompatible with its purpose. In treating of this phase of the subject we must consider marriage as an institution affecting not this or that individual but the human race. Also we must keep in mind that there is no law or institution among mankind that does not cause some individuals pain, loss, or hardship of one kind or another. If we abolished a thing because of its abuses or occasional hardships we should have to abolish every law and every institution in the world. There is nothing in the whole world, no matter how good it be, that is not subject to abuse; and nothing no matter how beneficial it be that does not occasion suffering or loss to some individuals.

Divorce with right to re-marry has done more to break up families than all the difficulties and differences that occur in family life. Man is fickle. When he pledges his troth to be faithful to the maiden he takes in marriage he means it. But the heart of man is restless. Man seeks novelty. A new face captivates him. Infatuated by a new love he not only loses his love for her to whom he pledged it, but begins to hate her because she is an obstacle to his new attraction.

Married life offers no immunity to the cares,

responsibilities and misunderstandings of life. Divorce does not remedy marriage evils but multiplies them. Permanency of the marriage bond has undoubtedly many undesirable consequences, but they are as nothing compared with the dreadful evils of divorce with re-marriage. The Church legislates for mankind. Every legislation which makes for the general good, occasions hardship in individual cases. The pure-food law may at times cause severe and unmerited loss to an individual concern or person but it safeguards the people.

In military affairs the interests of the individual soldier must be subordinated to those of the army. In matters of health the individual must be secondary to the public, as we see when a person is quarantined or otherwise inconvenienced for the sake of the general good. The marriage of one to one, and the permanence of the bond until death severs it, may cause individual hardship in specific cases. That is the nature of everything human. But it can be truly said that polygamy and divorce have wrought far more suffering on mankind than has monogamous and permanent marriage.

The mistake that many make is to think that marriage changes people's nature, and that in matrimony one must not expect the difficulties inherent in every department of life. If a man or woman have an affinity outside wedlock it is only natural that marriage relations will become strained. A man or woman in love with another does not have to look far or long to find incompatibility. But if they know that no future marriage is possible during the lifetime of either, they bear patiently the shortcomings of each other and eventually become congenial or at least bearable to each other.

Those who plead hardship or incompatibility as cause for divorce act differently towards marriage from what they do to everything else in life. Suppose one pleaded hardships as a cause for not keeping one's word of honor. Yet no word of honor equals the marriage vow. Suppose one pleaded hardship for not paying the income tax!

It is a matter of experience that some Catholics who have been married have had the marriage set aside and have re-married. How explain this in view of the Catholic doctrine of the indissolubility of marriage? To understand this we need to know just what constitutes a marriage. It may be said at the outset that among Christians no consummated valid marriage has ever been annulled, and never can be annulled.

A contract must be entered into freely. If

force or fear be employed in a civil contract, it is null. Under intimidation a person may do almost anything. The Church decrees that both parties to the marriage contract must be free. If it can be established that the marriage was forced by violence or unlawful threats, it is no marriage.

When the Roman Rota declared that the Marlborough-Vanderbilt marriage was null and void because of coercion, unusual interest and considerable misunderstanding was created. Annulment is not divorce. Divorce is the dissolution of the marriage bond. Annulment is the declaration that no such bond existed. The Catholic Church in the case of a consummated Christian marriage, has never granted a divorce with right to re-marry. It has declared many annulments of marriages. Every time a civil court sets aside a contract by declaring it null and void, it pronounces an annulment. The civil court does not break a contract by annulling it but simply affirms that the agreement in question was no contract at all.

Marriage is a contract. Christ elevated the Christian marriage contract to the dignity of a Sacrament but it remains essentially a contract. By the marriage ceremony the contracting parties mutually dispose of what is of most consequence to each, namely their own persons. The very nature of a contract requires that what one disposes of must be one's own, and that one must be free to dispose of it or to retain it.

A lack of free consent would invalidate a marriage even if the Catholic Church never existed. Natural justice and natural law demand that a person be free in executing a contract. In any civilized country, if a person were coerced into signing a civil contract, as Consuelo Vanderbilt was coerced in her marriage contract, the courts would nullify it.

It may seem to some people that to annul a marriage because of the absence of free consent is to open the door to laxity. But it must be remembered that the existence of coercion must be proved beyond a shadow of doubt. The testimony of the coerced party must be established by unquestionable corroboration. Annulment, far from letting down the bars of Christian marriage, makes stronger than ever the barrier to divorce. The Church which has annulled the marriage bond of Marlborough's invalid marriage suffered the loss of England to the Faith rather than break the bond of the valid marriage of her king.

CHAPTER XII

BIRTH CONTROL

BIRTH control was termed by Theodore Roosevelt race-suicide. The human race has a life as well as the individual. If birth control were practised universally the human race would perish. In sections of our own country where birth control has been in vogue the people have died out and given place to strangers. Birth control is nature perversion. It employs natural faculties in a way not only not intended by nature but contrary to nature's purposes. It defeats the plan of the Author of Nature as far as the creature can interfere with the plans of the Creator.

When we speak of birth control we mean artificial interference with the processes of nature. There is birth control and birth control. Persons who do not marry limit births. Married persons who practise self-control in sexual relations limit births. But the term birth control is not applied to either of these classes. The birth control which nature condemns is the use of a natural faculty contrary to nature's purposes.

An example may enable us to understand the unnaturalness of birth control. If a person were to eat just for the gratification of eating, and would not allow the food to pass into the stomach but would eject it in some way, he would soon starve to death. He would be guilty of suicide. This is just what birth control tends to do to the human race by contraceptive methods.

Birth control by the use of contraceptives is evil because it is nature perversion. Unmarried adults limit birth supply by refraining from marriage; which is their privilege. A person is free to make a contract but not free to play fast and loose with it when made. It may be objected that births are limited just as much by persons not marrying as by birth control in marriage. This is true, but while it is criminal to violate the nature of a contract it is not criminal to abstain from making a contract.

It may further be objected that married persons who practise self-control limit offspring. This is likewise true, but it is one thing to wreck an automobile while on a joy-ride, violating the law; quite another thing to have it wrecked while driving carefully and observing the law. The joy-rider is a criminal, not so the careful driver, even though the consequence in both cases be the same.

Nature will take care of the perpetuation of the human race, but this does not lessen the guilt of those who pervert nature. Birth control is wrong in itself, even if detriment never followed; just as stealing is wrong even though it should not absolutely ruin the victim.

Some defend birth control by saying that their purpose is not to prevent offspring but to limit the number to one or two. If a thing is evil it is not changed by more or less. It is wrong to steal whether the sum be two hundred dollars or two hundred thousand dollars. Birth control is a perversion of nature and immoral whether it be practised once or often.

The only reason why birth control does not actually destroy the human race is because nature destroys birth controllers. Prof. S. J. Holmes of the University of California, says: "Intelligence has outwitted nature in the matter of regulating the birth supply, but nature gets her revenge by extinguishing her adversary." This is why Roosevelt termed birth control race-suicide. Prof. Holmes, as we have seen, called birth controllers the enemies or adversaries of nature. Birth control is perversion of nature, it is a sin against nature, and in the end meets with dreadful penalties.

Nature attaches gratification to certain natural functions in order to assure their exercise. Eating, which is necessary to sustain life, gratifies the palate. Bodily exercise gives physical and mental exhilaration. Sleep is grateful to tired minds and bodies. If sleep, exercise and eating were not associated with pleasure, people might so neglect themselves that before they were conscious of the neglect they might collapse beyond restoration. So with regard to the sexual act whose natural purpose is to perpetuate the life of the race. Nature has attached a gratification to it in order to assure its exercise.

The responsibilities of bringing up children and providing for them are so many and great, that unless the sex urge strongly impelled people to the procreative act no children would be born into the world, and the human race would perish. Even as it is there are not a few people of both sexes who have an aversion to cohabitation. Unless nature powerfully attracted the sexes to intimate relationship the family would die out. A wise Creator has wisely provided for the perpetuation of mankind.

Here the birth controllers may say that they, too, advocate the perpetuation of the race but in a way that will be for its betterment. They affirm that fewer children mean a better world. They argue that they can provide nicely for one or two children but not for more. In certain parts of New England this plan was put into operation, with the result that soon there were few or no descendants of those who adopted it.

Some advocates of birth control affirm that what they intend is a better race. But if a man wants a better automobile he may not violate the laws of the State or of property in order to get it. There are other ways of bettering one's condition than by breaking the law. The thief wants better things than he has. That does not justify him in stealing.

Others plead poverty as a reason for birth control. But it is not the poor that practise this vice but the rich mainly. Birth controllers maintain that they can do more for their children if they be few in number. So could a man do more to dress his family if he refused to pay his bills. Nature prompts all mankind to better their condition, but by legitimate means. There are other ways of bettering offspring than by violating nature's laws.

Moreover the pampered children of birth controllers are not as a rule superior nor equal to children of large families. Frequently the pampered children of birth controllers turn out to be social parasites, or worthless degenerates, to the sorrow and often to the mortal anguish of their parents. These spoiled children are not able to compete with the hardy offspring of large families. Sir John Robertson, M.D., a high authority in the matter, says: "It is very questionable whether the members of large families do not make better citizens than the members of families of one or two only. . . . The laborer with a family of five or six children is on the whole better off and lives a happier life than the laborer without a family or with a family of one or two only." (Official Reports of the City of Birmingham, England, 1924.) A child in a large family receives a training in self-reliance, unselfishness and manliness which the offspring of birth controllers seldom or never acquire. But apart from all this, even if children were bettered by the practice of this unnatural vice by their parents, it would be the same as enriching them by unlawful means. No honorable man wants to be made wealthier by crime.

Some people seek to justify birth control by saying that they desire to better the human race. Fewer but better children make for a better world, they argue. Birth controllers are not solicitous for the race but for their own comfort and welfare. They are shirkers. They know that birth control instead of making the race better makes it disappear. A community which limits offspring to one or two children will in a few generations completely vanish. As Prof. Holmes has said, nature takes her revenge on birth controllers by destroying them. Advocates of birth control on the plea of bettering the race are refuted by nature herself.

The arguments of birth controllers are camouflage. Instead of admitting that they are practising this vice in order to serve their own pleasure and immediate advantage they try to throw dust into the eyes of people by affirming that they are solicitous for others. Instead of being willing to make the sacrifices and efforts required to bring up the children whom nature would ordinarily give them, they pervert nature. They are not good sports. They do not play the game fair. They want all the thrills but none of the knocks of the game.

Instead of birth control there is a legitimate way of restricting birth, and that is by self-control, which people must practise in every other sphere of life. If a man wants an automobile, and is not willing to pay for it, he goes without.

By birth control principles he would violate the law to get it.

Birth control degrades those who practise it. No less an authority than Dr. Howard A. Kelly, professor of gynecology, Johns Hopkins University, says: "All meddling with sex relations to secure facultative sterility degrades the wife to the level of a prostitute. . . . There is no right or decent way of controlling births but by total abstinence." (Harpers Weekly, Oct. 16th., 1916.) Birth controllers in their sane moments despise themselves. Some may be dead to shame in this matter, but that only makes them more degraded. Prof. Paul Bureau, University of Paris, states: "Whether he likes it or not every adult who claims the right to unfruitful sexual relationships and that the sexual power with which he is endowed is for his own pleasure and enjoyment, spreads through society the seeds of disintegration and disorder." (L'Indiscipline des Moeurs, 1924.)

Self-control, not birth control, needs to be inculcated. Dr. Paul Dubois, University of Berne, affirms: "There are more neurastheniacs among those who give free-rein to their passions than among those who know how to escape the yoke of animality."

Catholics refuse to practise birth control because God condemns it. Birth control is a deadly sin. A Catholic can not receive the Sacraments of the Church and practise this unnatural vice. The Church condemns it because nature and God condemn it. The Bible tells us that for committing this sin Onan was struck dead: "The Lord slew him, because he did a detestable thing." (Gen. xxxviii. 10.) God's laws are not subject to man's approval or pleasure. Nature's laws are God's laws.

At times it may be a hardship to observe God's laws with regard to marriage. But hardship does not excuse from observance of the State law. Taxes are a hardship. Every law at times is burdensome. We have to make sacrifices and exercise restraint in every department of life. Marriage is no exception.

Because birth controllers are not punished instantly it does not mean that they go free. Nature, as well as God, has her own time and way of vindicating herself. We may defy God if we will. He made us free. He will not physically force us to serve Him. But we violate His law at our own peril. We never know how or when He will deal with those who do not respect His authority.

Duty to the state often requires that we risk health, possessions, and even life. It was not agreeable to pay war taxes, nor to go over-seas to face deadly gas and shells, nor to go "over the top" on the battle line. But duty to country demanded this. We are more the subjects of God than of the State. At times God's service may require the sacrifice of fortune, health or life. But Christ has said: "He that shall lose his life for My sake, shall find it. For what doth it profit a man, if he gain the whole world, and suffer the loss of his own soul? Or what exchange shall a man give for his soul? For the Son of Man shall come in the glory of His Father with His angels: and then will He render to every man according to his works." (Mt. xvi. 25-27.)

But, in the words of Scripture, "The fool hath said in his heart: There is no God." (Ps. xiii. 1.) To-day there are not a few who play fast and loose with nature as if there were no God. But God will not be mocked. In His own time and way He will assert His authority. Blessed shall we be, if when we meet God face to face, it will be to hear from Him the words of welcome which will make us His beloved children forever in the kingdom He has prepared for them that love Him. If we are faithful subjects of God here, we shall be His beloved children hereafter. Obedience to God's law is the title to everlasting membership in the divine family.

CHAPTER XIII

FUTURE LIFE

THE most important subject that concerns man is future life. If I am to terminate my career *forever* when the grave receives me, I shall live for this life only; I shall regulate my conduct with an eye to present consequences only; right and wrong will have no other meaning for me than gain or loss; the natural law will be a myth; I will be a high-grade animal, controlling my actions by cunning or power.

The chief reason why crime is so rampant now is because for the past generation man has been taught that he is but a high-class animal, and that his end will be like the animal's. Materialism is beginning to reap the harvest of its sowing. If man be a material being only, of course he is governed by physical laws and can no more control his conduct than can a lion control its instinct for killing its prey. But man is more than an animal. He has something which no animal has—namely, intelligence.

Animals have wonderful qualities; in some respects animals surpass man. The eagle can see farther than man; the elephant is stronger than man; the greyhound can outrun man. But man, by reason of his intelligence, can invent a telescope by which he sees farther than the eagle; he can make machinery to do the work of a thousand elephants; and, he can build speed machines which outstrip the fleetest creature of land or air.

Animals are ruled by iron instinct. A bird with some fragments of waste can build a nest which no human hand could construct. But a bird always build the same kind of nest. Its first nest is the same as its last. A bird flies perfectly although it knows nothing about aviation. Animals may be trained by man to do things which appear to be intelligent, but which represent only the intelligence of man which has been superimposed on them.

Why do I touch on this subject of animal instinct? Because some superficial thinkers assert that the instinct of animals is the same as the intelligence of man, and that consequently man's final destiny is no different from that of the animal. But man's mind is as different from that of the animal as gold is from brass. You may polish brass and get it to resemble gold but you can not make it gold.

Man's mind is a different substance from that of the animal. Man's mind is spiritual, the animal's is material. An animal can not invent, nor compose, nor deal with anything that is beyond the reach of the senses. The mind of the animal is tied down to what is material. Man's mind reaches out beyond the realm of material things and deals with what is abstract. I have not time to develop this thought, let me say just this: man's mind can deal with things which do not actually exist. He can deal with possibilities, with future conditions, with abstract ideas.

It is man's spiritual nature which makes him lord of creation. Man is weaker than the horse but he makes the horse do his work. Man is not as strong as the elephant yet with a few sticks of dynamite he can exert more power than a thousand elephants. The faculty in man which thinks, invents, composes, is his soul. It has activities which do not depend on matter, which transcend matter. Such a faculty we designate as spiritual. It has no parts.

The mind of man—because it has no parts, because it is spiritual—can reflect perfectly on itself which no material substance can do. For instance, while I am thinking I can reflect on my thoughts, my mind can examine itself, pass judgment on itself. I myself can deliberately analyze myself. This power belongs to man alone of all the beings of this world. The reason why my mind can perfectly turn itself back on itself is because it has no parts. If it had parts it could turn one part on another, but not its whole self on its whole self as the mind does when it analyzes itself. It is because the soul of man has no parts that it can not die.

What do we mean by death? Death means the dissolution of a being, the breaking up of something that exists, in such a way that the thing no longer exists as it was before. For instance, when an animal dies it is no longer an animal but a carcass. Death has destroyed the element which gave unity to the various parts of the animal, and these parts—being no longer sustained—begin to break up and disappear into various gases and elements. When man dies, his material part—like the body of the animal—begins to disintegrate and change into other material elements. But the soul—not having parts—can not break up. Moreover not being dependent on matter for its activities, it can exist apart from matter, independent of matter, and so after death of the body it continues its spiritual life. This is a proof from metaphysics or philosophy that the soul lives on.

There are other proofs that the soul is immortal. Every instinct of man has something in nature to satisfy its craving. Hunger is satisfied by food; thirst is satisfied by water. Man's craving for happiness is an instinct as much as is his desire for food. The Creator did not give us the instinct for happiness without the possibility of our attaining happiness. But in this life no one can satisfy his instinct for happiness, so there must be a place beyond where it can be satisfied, for the Creator does not create an instinct without an object to satisfy it.

Moreover the Creator Who gave us our sense of justice must Himself be just. But frequently there is little or no justice on earth. The powerful, the shrewd, the unscrupulous often defy justice. The world is strewn with the victims of injustice. Unless there is a future life where justice will rectify the wrongs of this life we should have to conclude that God was indifferent to right and wrong. Our sense of justice came from the Author of Nature. We may therefore give the Creator credit for at least as much justice as He has bestowed upon His creature. So we know that there is a future life where God will justify His dealings with mankind.

But even if we have no philosophical grounds for believing in a future life we have the word of God for it, which is much better than all human speculation. God speaks to us by His holy prophet, Job: "I know that my Redeemer liveth, and in the last day I shall rise out of the earth. And I shall be clothed again with my skin, and in my flesh I shall see my God. . . . This my hope is laid up in my bosom." (Job xix. 25-27.) Christ Himself proclaimed: "I am the resurrection and the life: he that believeth in Me, although he be dead, shall live: and every one that liveth, and believeth in Me, shall not die forever." (Jn. xi. 25, 26.)

God not only proclaims that there is a future life but that the future life will be what we make it. "The hour cometh, wherein all that are in the grave shall hear the voice of the Son of God. And they that have done good things, shall come forth unto the resurrection of life; but they that have done evil, unto the resurrection of judgment." (Jn. v. 28, 29.) It is because man's soul is immortal that Christ said: "What shall a man give in exchange for his soul?" (Mk. viii. 37.) He Who created man and gave him his soul could name nothing that was fair exchange for the soul. Hence He also said again: "What shall it profit a man, if he gain the whole world, and suffer the loss of his soul?" (Mk. viii. 36.)

But the greatest proof of the future life and the value of the human soul is that Christ died on the cross that we might live forever. Calvary has no meaning if there be no future life. In fact life itself has no meaning if it end with the grave. This present life is hardly life at all, but rather a living death since we begin to die as soon as we are born. Christ gave His life that we might have life, unending life, real life, a share in His own divine life.

"To as many as receive Him He gives them the power to become the children of God." (Jn. i. 12.) That is the purpose of life,—to give us power to share in the very life of God. In Christ's own words: "They that shall be accounted worthy of that world, and of the resurrection from the dead. . . . can die no more: for they are equal to the angels, and are the children of God." (Lk. xx. 35, 36.)

That is the destiny of man if he will use this life as God directs. That makes life worth while no matter how dark the way or heavy the burden for it leads to the home of Our Heavenly Father where for all eternity we shall enjoy the life that knows no pain, no care, no uncertainty, no separation from dear ones, no end. The happiest life here is misery compared with the life of glory awaiting those who win the crown of immortal blessedness with God. "Eye hath not seen, nor ear heard, nor hath it entered into heart of man to conceive the things that God hath prepared for them that love Him."

CHAPTER XIV

THE NATURE OF THE MASS

IF the Mass be not a divine oblation it is idolatry. If the Mass be not essentially the same Sacrifice as that of the Cross Christianity is blasphemy. We know that the Mass is not idolatry and that Christianity is not blasphemy. We know that when Christ at the Last Supper declared that He gave His Body and Blood as an oblation that the oblation was consummated the following day by the Sacrifice of Calvary.

But although we believe that the Mass is essentially the same Sacrifice as that of the Cross, are we able to explain the Mass intelligently to those who differ from us? Suppose an earnest inquirer were to ask us: "How can Christ, Who was sacrificed on Calvary, be sacrificed again in the Mass?" What should we say to this? St. Paul tells us that we should be able to give a reason for our belief. Although our religion is called Our Holy Faith, it does not mean that we believe blindly. Not that we understand the mysteries of God's Revelation, but that we do know why we believe them. No matter how incomprehensible the mysteries of Faith be they have been revealed by God Who is Truth itself, and they cannot be unreasonable.

It is one thing for a statement to be incomprehensible, quite another for it to be unreasonable. For instance, it is incomprehensible to us how the bread we eat becomes our flesh and blood. But we know it, although we do not comprehend it. We know it on evidence. We experience the change in our very bodies.

Besides accepting the incomprehensible on the evidence of our senses, we also accept it on the authority of those in whom we have faith. To the generality of mankind it is incomprehensible that the earth, which seems so stationary, is in constant motion both rotary and through space; yet it is believed by the majority of mankind because of faith in the scientific knowledge of those who declare it. This faith is based on the fact that astronomers are worthy of credit because they have given evidence of trustworthiness in various matters that the average person can verify.

It is so with Christian Faith. Christians accept the doctrine of Christ because He gave evidence that He was absolutely trustworthy. When He proclaimed that He was God He substantiated His claim by doing what God alone could do. "If you do not believe Me," He said, "at least believe the works which I do, they give testimony of Me." (Jn. v. 36.) Seekers after truth employ their reason to ascertain if Christ be God, and when they are satisfied that He is God, it is most reasonable to believe what He says, since God is Truth.

Faith is therefore not blind, but most reasonable. We do not comprehend God's works, much less should we expect to comprehend Himself. But this much we comprehend that if He speaks He is to be believed, even if what He declares be beyond our comprehension. So at the Last Supper when Christ said: "This is My Body," we believe what He said, although we do not comprehend how it is so. When furthermore He said: "This is My Body, which is given for you," we believe that He then made an oblation of Himself for us. He did not explain how this oblation was effected, but the next day on Calvary He completed the oblation by the Sacrifice of the Cross.

But how is the Mass the same Sacrifice as that of the Cross? Before we answer this question let us reflect a little on the Sacrifice offered on Calvary. On Calvary Christ was immolated.

His Body was mangled and His Blood flowed freely. It is clear that the Victim of the Cross was sacrificed; but how is the Mass a sacrifice? In the Mass where is the victim, where is the oblation? Without a victim there can be no sacrifice, without a victim there can be no oblation. Christ was immolated once for all. He is now in glory. He can die no more. How then can He be sacrificed on the altar? The Mass is the renewal of the Sacrifice of Calvary; but how is the glorious, risen Christ sacrificed again?

Although the Sacrifice of the Mass is a mystery which we accept on God's word, it can not be a contradiction, it can not be unreasonable. We may seek, therefore, to understand how the Mass is a true sacrifice, the same as that of the Cross, in everything except the manner in which it is offered.

The Mass is an action which accomplishes primarily two things, namely: it shows the death of the Lord, and offers the immolated Christ a sacrifice to the Eternal Father. St. Peter Canisius says: "The Sacrifice of the Mass, rightly understood, is both a representation—at once holy and living, and an offering—bloodless yet actual, of the passion of the Lord and of the bloodstained Sacrifice which was offered for us on the Cross." (Canisius' Catechism.) Always the Mass shows the death of the Lord, and is besides an oblation—real, though bloodless—of Christ's passion and death. The Mass besides *representing* the Sacrifice of the Cross also *offers* unto God the Sacrifice of the Cross. What the Mass represents—namely, the death of Christ—that it offers as a sacrifice. The Mass, therefore, is both a representation of Christ immolated for us on the Cross, and the oblation of the immolated Christ as a sacrifice.

The Mass as the representation of Christ's passion, and the oblation of His Body and Blood is recorded by St. Paul addressing the Corinthians: "The Lord Jesus, the same night in which He was betrayed, took bread, and giving thanks, broke, and said: Take ye, and eat: this is My Body, which shall be delivered for you: this do for the commemoration of Me. In like manner also the Chalice, after He had supped, saying: This Chalice is the New Testament in My Blood: this do ye, as often as you shall drink, for the commemoration of Me. For as often as you shall eat this Bread, and drink the Chalice, you shall show the death of the Lord, until He come." (I Cor. xi. 23-26.) Christ wanted His followers to have a perpetual reminder of what He suffered for them. For this reason He commanded the apostles to do in memory of Him what they had seen Him do at the Last Supper: "Do this for the commemoration of Me."

But the passion of Christ was something more than suffering and death. It was besides, or rather principally, a sacrifice.

Now what is a sacrifice? It is the offering of something of value by destruction or privation to another who accepts it. In the Old Testament there were various sacrifices. Whether they were possessions donated to God's service, or victims slain, always these sacrifices implied giving up something of value and their acceptance by Almighty God.

On the Cross Christ offered to His heavenly Father what was of most value to Him—namely, His life. He sacrificed His life that we might have eternal life, and the Eternal Father in accepting this sacrifice put it into the power of each one of us to become a child of God. "To as many as received Him, He gave them the power to become the sons of God." (Jn. i. 12.)

And now the question arises, how does Christ sacrifice Himself in the Mass? For we hold, that, since the Mass is essentially the same Sacrifice as Calvary, Christ Himself offers Himself in the Mass an oblation to Almighty God. If the Mass is a renewal of the crucifixion there must be a divine victim and an oblation of the victim. By the consecration at Mass we have both Victim and oblation. Let us see how this is effected.

First of all, at Mass Christ is the Sacrificing Priest. The celebrant of Mass represents Christ, and is the human instrument that Christ uses to perform the sacrifice. Christ began the sacrifice of Himself not on the Cross but at the Last Supper when He willed to be slain: "This is My Body, which is given for you. . . . This is My Blood, which shall be shed for you." (Lk. xxii. 19, 20.) The executioners at the crucifixion were the means of effecting the sacrifice which Christ made when at the Last Supper He willed to die for us. He Himself, since He freely offered Himself to death (Jn. x. 17), was the real Sacrificing Priest, the executioners being the instruments or human means of carrying out the sacrifice.

It is for this reason that Christ is called by St. Paul "a high-priest according to the order of Melchisedech." (Heb. v. 10.) Melchisedech sacrificed to Almighty God by the clean oblation of bread and wine. The Mass is the perpetual clean oblation, bread and wine being the species of the sacrifice. The psalmist, referring to the priesthood of Christ, exclaims: "Thou art a priest forever according to the order of Melchisedech." (Ps. cix. 4.) Christ, as the real Sacrificing Priest in the Mass, is the priest forever.

At Mass Christ is the One Who offers the sacrifice, employing the celebrant as the means of accomplishing it. Hence at the consecration the priest does *not* say: "This is *the Body of Christ"*; but, speaking for Christ, says: "This is *My* Body." By these words at the consecration of the Mass, the bread becomes the Body of Christ. Since where Christ's Body is there He is, by the first consecration Christ becomes present on the altar.

Now comes the showing of the death of Christ. On the Cross Jesus shed His Blood for us, thus giving up His life for our salvation. By the second consecration—that of the wine—the death of Christ is shown. For by the consecrations of the wine the Chalice then contains the Blood of Christ and there is mystically represented that separation of Christ's Blood from His Body which caused His death on the Cross. It is thus that the Mass is a memorial or reminder of Christ's death—the mystical separation of Body and Blood, represented by the second consecration, showing the death of the Saviour.

But death is not necessarily a sacrifice. Not all those who die sacrifice their lives. Sacrifice of life means freely offering oneself to death, as when a soldier knowing that certain death awaits an undertaking nevertheless volunteers for it.

Christ freely offered Himself for the cruel death His enemies inflicted on Him. "I lay down My life, that I may take it up again. No man taketh it away from Me: but I lay it down of Myself." (Jn. x. 17, 18.) In the Mass He again freely offers Himself a victim through the priest. And how? By the very words which He employed when first offering Himself to be immolated. At the Last Supper He gave Himself a victim to be immolated, His death on the following day being the consummation of that offering. In the Mass He offers Himself again as the Victim that was immolated on Calvary—renewing the Sacrifice.

But it may be asked, how can Christ Who is now in glory be a sacrificial victim? Christ can die no more. How then can He be offered as a sacrificial victim in the Mass?

The actual shedding of blood is not an essential part of sacrifice. The same blood, once previously offered up in sacrifice, may again be offered up to constitute a second distinct sacrifice. Thus the Jewish high-priest, on the solemn festival of expiation, did not immolate a fresh victim within the holy of holies, but carried with him, within the veil, the blood of the victim that had been previously shed on the altar of holocausts, and offered it up a second time to accomplish atonement. This second offering constituted of itself a sacrifice, although not accompanied with the shedding of blood.

In like manner Jesus does not die a second time on our altars, but the Sacrifice which He made once for all on the Cross He continually renews upon the altar, by offering up again the Victim slain once for all on Calvary; thus constituting the Sacrifice of the Cross and that of the Mass one and the same Sacrifice. The Sacrifice which was first offered at the Last Supper, and then consummated on the Cross, is perpetuated on the altars of the Church. At the Last Supper Christ offered Himself a victim to be immolated. On the Cross He was immolated. In the Mass that immolated Victim is offered again. This makes the Mass a sacrifice, because in the Mass Christ offers to Almighty God the Victim once slain, but now perpetually living and glorified.

It is thus that the Mass renews the Sacrifice of the Cross. Until the end of time the Mass will be offered as an infinite oblation to the

Divine Majesty for man's salvation and sanctification. The "Imitation of Christ" says: "The visible priest is but the minister of Christ using the words of Christ, by the command and institution of Christ." (Bk. iv. 5.) The Sacrifice of the Cross redeemed us. The Sacrifice of the Mass gives to succeeding generations the blessing of participating most beneficially in the Sacrifice of Calvary. The Sacrifice of the Cross was of infinite value, its effects can never be exhausted.

By the Mass the fruits of Redemption are most effectually imparted to mankind. For the Mass, besides showing the death of the Lord, and offering up the divine Victim as a sacrifice, is also the means of uniting us intimately with Our Redeemer. When at Mass we receive Holy Communion we partake of the Eucharist, the Sacrament of Christ's Body and Blood.

To sum up, therefore, let it be repeated that the same Sacrifice that was offered on Calvary by the shedding of blood is offered on our altars in an unbloody manner. In everything except the manner of offering, the Mass is the same Sacrifice as that of the Cross. Christ is the Lamb of God Who was slain for the redemption of the world. He is the perpetual Victim, for He is the Lamb of God even in the Kingdom of Glory.

As the perpetual Lamb of God He is offered daily at Mass throughout the world from the rising of the sun until its going down, thus fulfilling the prophecy of Malachias. "From the rising of the sun even to the going down, My name is great among the Gentiles, and in every place there is sacrifice, and there is offered a clean oblation." (Mal. i. 11.)

The Holy Sacrifice of the Mass is the highest act of worship that can be paid to Almighty God. It is the worship instituted by Jesus Christ Himself. It is the most sacred action that can be performed on this earth. When we assist at Mass we stand at the foot of the Cross.

(*For those interested in a more detailed explanation of the Mass, Father Scott's book "The Holy Sacrifice of the Mass" will be interesting and informing.—Publisher's Note.*)

CHAPTER XV

CHURCH AND STATE

WHEN the phrase *Church and State* is used it is generally in reference to the Catholic Church and a Christian State. By the Catholic Church is meant that institution founded by Jesus Christ the Son of God, and by Him guaranteed immunity from error in teaching revealed truth, and perpetuity of existence. It is necessary to keep this idea of the Catholic Church in mind in order rightly to understand the relationship between Church and State.

Catholics firmly believe—and are willing to die for their belief—that the Church established by Jesus Christ cannot teach error with regard to faith or morals. They believe that once the Church speaks authoritatively on these matters, it is the same as if God has spoken. For this belief literally millions of martyrs have in the past laid down their lives; and for this belief millions are ready at present to give their life, if necessary. Catholics believe that the

Church founded by Jesus Christ, and by Him guaranteed to last until the end of the world, is a divine compass of truth which directs man unerringly over the sea of mortal life to the shores of eternal life. Catholics believe that what Christ taught is as true as God, and that His teaching was intended for mankind for all time.

Christ did not write His teaching in a book, but instead established a Living Voice which He called His Church, of which He said: "He that heareth you, heareth Me." (Lk. x. 16.) Christ declared of Himself that He was "The Light of the World." (Jn. viii. 12.) Catholics regard the Church as that Light and strive to walk by its illumination.

The Church founded by Christ, and which by His solemn promise is now in the world an unerring teacher of His truth, is a perfect society. By a *perfect society* is meant one which has in itself, independently of every other institution, everything necessary for its existence and functioning. The purpose of Christ's Church is to direct man to eternal life, and to aid him to attain that blessed end. She declares that although man must live in this world he is not to live altogether for it. The grave is not the goal but starting point of man. The mission of the Church of Christ is to guide man securely to the attainment of his last end. She declares with her divine Founder: "What doth it profit a man, if he gain the whole world, and suffer the loss of his own soul?" (Mt. xvi. 26.)

But although Christ's Church makes man's main purpose in life the salvation of his immortal soul, she does not neglect his temporal welfare. In point of fact, in proportion as man directs his life by the truth will he be doing what is most advantageous for his real welfare even in the present life. However the main purpose of the religion of Jesus Christ is not worldly welfare but everlasting happiness. Christ Himself was not rich, nor did He have a long life, nor was He distinguished by worldly honors. On the contrary He was poor, He died in early manhood, and He was reputed with the wicked. But He also rose gloriously from the tomb, and opened the gates of everlasting life and bliss to all who follow Him. The Church of Christ therefore has for her object to make mankind followers of her divine Founder, in order that where He reigns in glory, there they also may dwell who live by Him and for Him. In brief, therefore, the mission of the Church of Christ is to be man's guide to heaven.

The Catholic Church owes her Charter to no human government nor to any human agency.

She was founded and chartered by our divine Lord Himself: "All power is given to Me in heaven and on earth; going therefore, teach ye all nations . . . teaching them to observe all things whatsoever I have commanded you: and behold I am with you all days, even to the end of the world." (Mt. xxviii. 18-20.) By this commission given her by her divine Founder the mission of the Church is to all nations.

From the fact that the Church has for its field the whole world, it necessarily follows that her subjects will also be subjects of various governments. This is what constitutes the problem of Church and State. Persons of various countries owe allegiance to their national government. If they become Christians they also owe allegiance to the Church of Christ. Christians, thus owing allegiance to both Church and State, find themselves subjects of both a spiritual and a temporal power. Ordinarily there is no difficulty under this twofold allegiance. Rather the Church by her ministration helps her subjects to be good citizens of the State; and the State by maintaining order and security helps the Church to carry on her work.

The ideal condition for the Christian Church is cooperation with a Christian government. But the Church rarely finds herself in the ideal condition. She has been obliged to carry on her mission under every form of government, and under every condition of human society, from the highly civilized nations of Christendom to the savage tribes of newly discovered lands. When we speak of union of Church and State we speak of an ideal condition. The cooperation of a Christian State with the Christian Church is ideally the best condition under which the Church can work for society and guide mankind to everlasting welfare.

Whenever the Church advocates union of Church and State it is always under the presumption that the State's religion is the same as that of the Church. In a government like that of the United States the Church would not advocate union of Church and State because the Constitution of the United States proclaims that there should be no religious discrimination. There would be discrimination if the Catholic Church were made the State Church. Since the Catholic Church is the greatest upholder of authority in the world, she would not advocate a condition which would violate legitimate constitutional government. The Catholic Church would be false to her teaching if she sought to act contrary to rightly established authority. Legitimate governments everywhere and of every kind realize that the Catholic Church is their firmest support. Rarely does the Church find ideal conditions. That is why union of Church and State is so infrequent.

Union of Church and State can not take place unless the State wants it. We may dismiss, therefore, this phase of the matter by saying that union of Church and State depends, as an actual fact, on the State; and that consequently no nation need be alarmed about a condition of which itself is the master. In the past whenever union of Church and State existed it was because the State realized that it was for its own best welfare. Again let it be said, finally and emphatically, that there can be no union of Church and State except the State desire it.

Another phase of Church and State concerns what is termed *divided allegiance to the two powers*—spiritual and temporal. The case is stated as follows. Suppose the Church command what the State forbids; what must the subjects of the Church do under such circumstances? The answer to this is plain. The State must be obeyed in everything except what is against the law of God. No State can oblige a man to offend his Creator. If a government demand that its subjects violate their conscience, how can it expect those who are disloyal to God to be loyal to the State? The United States Government since its foundation has not found its Catholic subjects divided in allegiance between Church and State. Mark Hanna, the political mentor of President McKinley, declared that the two firmest supports of authority in the United States were the United States Supreme Court and the Catholic Church. That does not look like divided allegiance.

But suppose that a State command what the Church forbids; what then? The answer is that given by the apostles to their persecutors, and by the martyrs to the pagan tyrants: "Judge ye, whether we should obey man rather than God." (Acts iv. 19.) Christ has said: "What doth it profit a man, if he gain the whole world, and suffer the loss of his own soul?" (Mt. xvi. 26.) If there be question, therefore, between worldly welfare and eternal salvation the Christian should never hesitate. Even if allegiance to God mean loss of life the Christian will gladly pay the price; for Christ, foreseeing such a possibility, has proclaimed: "He who loses his life for My sake, shall save it." (Lk. ix. 24.)

No state whose subjects are loyal to God need be concerned about their allegiance to legitimate authority. The more loyal a Catholic is to his Church the more loyal will he be to the State, as history attests. The better Catholic a man is the better citizen will he be. Our own country has had and will have no more staunch defenders than her Catholic subjects. The man who is true to God will not be false to country. Loyalty to Church is guarantee of loyalty to State.

"This is all very well," it may be objected, "but it does not touch the real problem of Church and State. Suppose the State considers its commands just and lawful, while the Church holds the opposite; which view is to prevail? The State is the supreme authority of the nation, and legislates for the general well-being of its subjects. It knows best what public welfare demands. The State's laws are made for national welfare. It is the best judge of the nation's needs and safeguards. Because the Church judges the State's laws as unjust or un-Christian does that make them so? Is the Church justified in sitting in judgment on the State? In a conflict between Church ethics and State ethics must the State give way to the Church?" This is really the crux of the problem of Church and State. Let me say briefly that if there should arise a subject of dispute between the Church and State the Church would meet the requirements of the State in everything compatible with her duty to God. No just government should demand more than that.

In conclusion let me say that no State can have better subjects than those who reverence God. It is impossible to be true to Christ and disloyal to Country. The State that fosters religion promotes patriotism. The Church is the firmest support of every government that has man's true welfare at heart. No State need doubt the loyalty of those who are loyal to God.

CHAPTER XVI

PURGATORY

THE doctrine of Purgatory, rightly understood, is one of the most reasonable and consoling truths of revealed religion. Luther saw so much to admire and approve in it that for a long time he hesitated about rejecting it. Finally he rejected it because it was distinctly Catholic.

Many modern Protestants, while avoiding the word *Purgatory,* teach the real doctrine of Purgatory. They call it the Middle State. Martensen, for instance, writes: "As no soul leaves this present existence in a fully complete and prepared state, we must suppose that there is an intermediate state, a realm of progressive development, in which souls are prepared for the final judgment." (Christian Dogmatics, Edinburgh, 1890, p. 457.) Other references: Farrar —"Mercy and Judgment"; and Campbell— "The Doctrines of the Middle State."

Another non-Catholic, Mallock, speaks as follows: "It is becoming fast recognized on all sides that Purgatory is the only doctrine that can bring a belief in future rewards and punishments into anything like accordance with our notion of what is just and reasonable. So far from its being a superfluous superstition, it is seen to be just what is demanded at once by reason and morality; and a belief in it to be not an intellectual assent only, but a partial harmonizing of the whole mortal ideal." (Is Life Worth Living? ch. xi. p. 290.)

It stands to reason that God is just. It is also evident that many of us depart from this life not altogether saints and yet not altogether sinners. Moreover, some who have been notoriously wicked repent at the last moment, and God has declared that He will not reject the penitent sinner. Such a penitent, although assured of God's forgiveness, must nevertheless atone for his lifelong transgressions. Unless there is a place beyond where atonement can be made, the death-bed penitent would entirely escape chastisement for sin.

It is true that Christ forgave the sins of the thief on the cross, and also remitted the chastisement of them. He may do that with every sinner if He so wills. But that is not His ordinary way, as we know from Scripture. God forgave David his sin but chastised him dreadfully nevertheless. So, too, He punished Moses and others after He had pronounced forgiveness of their sins.

We have, therefore, the fact that God is just and merciful, and also the fact that not all of us depart this life holy enough for companionship with God, and yet not wicked enough for perpetual banishment from His presence. Scripture declares that nothing defiled can enter heaven. They, therefore, who have lesser sins on their souls, or who have repented but not received chastisement in this life for their wickedness, must be made worthy of entrance into the all-holy presence of God in some place beyond this life. That is what is meant by the doctrine of Purgatory.

Purgatory may be defined as a place or condition of temporal punishment for those who, departing this life in God's grace, are not entirely free from lesser sins, or have not fully paid the satisfaction due to their transgressions. Christ Himself proclaimed that the sinner must pay the penalty of wrong-doing. He said of sinners: "Unless you shall do penance, you shall all likewise perish." (Lk. xiii. 3.)

How many sinners have done adequate penance for their offences? Christ, Who redeemed all mankind, did not thereby relieve us of doing our part for sin's atonement. By redemption He made it possible for the greatest sinner to obtain pardon, but on condition that the sinner make reparation as far as he is able. Some either neglect or have not the opportunity of making due satisfaction for their sins in this life; hence unless there is a place beyond where this can be done they can have no companionship with the all-holy God in the kingdom of the blessed.

Let us take, for example, the case of a man who has been dishonest all his life, even to the extent of depriving the widow and the orphan of their substance. Let us add to all this the crime of deliberate murder in order to obtain possession of another's goods. Now such a man is despicable in the sight of angels and men. Yet God's mercy is not closed against even such a malefactor. While there is life God's forgiveness may be had. Suppose such a one turns to God at the very last. God will forgive him if he truly repents. God, Who knows the heart, is the sole Judge in these matters. But if the guilt of sin is remitted by a merciful God, it does not follow that chastisement is not required by a just God. Such a sinner might indeed be forgiven, the guilt of his wickedness might be blotted out by the merits of Christ's redemption; but chastisement might be exacted by a long, a very long atonement in the life beyond the grave.

Some non-Catholics object to Purgatory because there is no specific mention of it in Scripture. There is no specific mention of the word Sunday in Scripture. The Sabbath is mentioned, but Sabbath means Saturday. Yet the Christians of almost all denominations worship on Sunday, not on Saturday. But although there is no specific mention of the word Purgatory in Scripture, there is specifically mentioned the very thing that Purgatory means. Purgatory means a place or condition of purification after this life. The Jews offered sacrifice for their deceased brethren. The high-priest in person performed the sacrificial rites for the dead. Now, unless there was a place such as Purgatory, sacrifice for the dead would be meaningless. For if there were only heaven or hell hereafter those in heaven would not need help, and those in hell could not profit by it. Consequently there must be a middle state which is temporary and purificatory. This we call Purgatory.

We read in Scripture that Judas Machabeus sent an offering to Jerusalem for the dead, because "It is therefore a holy and wholesome thought to pray for the dead, that they may be loosed from sins." (II Mach. xii. 46.) Even if this text were history only, and not Scripture, it would prove the reality of Purgatory since it shows that the Jewish people believed in prayer for the dead, and Christ did not correct that belief, as He was bound to do if it were erroneous.

But Christ Himself taught the doctrine of Purgatory; He declared that certain sins were not forgiven either here or hereafter. (Lk. xiii. 27.) This means that at least some sins are forgiven in the life beyond. That is the meaning of Purgatory. St. Paul also states that some will be saved yet so as by fire. (I Cor. iii. 15.) Hence from the very time of the apostles, sacrifice was offered for the souls of the departed. In the great central act of worship of the Apostolic Church, prayers for the dead were an integral part of the service. Even to-day we can obtain visible evidence of prayers for the dead by inspecting the tombs in the Catacombs.

The Church of Christ from her very origin taught the doctrine of Purgatory, and, what is more, exemplified the doctrine by her ritual and devotions. Christ guaranteed His Church against error. Consequently what His Church taught was true. If the Church of Christ taught what was false, Christ was not God, for God's promise cannot fail; and if Christ be not God all Christianity is false. Christ also promised that His Church should last forever. It was, therefore, in the world from His day, down to our own, and is in the world now. The only Church recognized as His from the beginning taught the doctrine of Purgatory. If, therefore, Purgatory is not true, His Church was not true, and Christianity is a deception or worse.

When Christ established His Church He endowed it with truth and perpetuity. His doctrine would have perished with His voice unless He had devised some means of transmitting it down the ages. Christ never wrote a line. He left nothing in a book. What He did leave was a living book—His Church—which was to be His voice in the world to the end of time. Christ spent years in instructing His apostles, and moreever sent upon them the Holy Ghost, Who recalled to them all His teaching and inspired them with all that they should do in their apostolic ministry. Hence it was that in the first apostolic decree we find these opening words: "It hath seemed good to the Holy Ghost and us." The early Church spoke in the name and with the authority of God. It was this early Church which established prayers for the dead, and made a commemoration of the dead an integral part of its solemn service, the Holy Sacrifice of the Mass.

Christian piety has always followed the faithful departed by prayer and alms, and especially by the Holy Sacrifice of the Altar. God's mercy is over all His works. Surely His mercy is manifest in the comforting doctrine of Purgatory, by which we know that in spite of minor transgressions, and sins forgiven but unsatisfied for, we may nevertheless hope to be made worthy to associate with God in that blessed kingdom which He has prepared for them that love Him.

When St. Monica, the mother of St. Augustine, felt that she was about to die she said to her son: "Lay this body of mine where thou wilt; one thing only I ask of thee, remember me, when I am gone, at the Holy Sacrifice of the Altar." Thus spoke one saint to another, in the first ages of Christianity.

One can not purchase one's way to heaven. In praying for the faithful departed we do so by way of suffrage or petition—that is, we offer our good works to God in their behalf, leaving it to Him to accept them for those for whom they are offered.

The doctrine of Purgatory is a great help to the living, since it enables them to practise charity in a high degree; and a consolation to the faithful departed, since it gives them hope that their period of probation may be shortened. "It is therefore a holy and wholesome thought to pray for the dead, that they may be loosed from their sins." (II Mach. xii. 46.)

CHAPTER XVII

HELL

HELL is the most dreadful doctrine of Christianity. The gentleness of Jesus seems to be incompatible with the teaching of eternal punishment. Christ was the kindest person who was ever in this world. Hell is the most dreadful idea that the mind of man can conceive. The character of Jesus seems to be a contradiction to the doctrine of hell. Yet if language have any meaning, Christ taught us that there is a hell. He not only taught that there is a hell but continually warned us against it.

A chain is no stronger than its weakest link. If one doctrine of Christ be false He is not God, and Christianity is a fraud. Revelation must be accepted in its entirety or altogether rejected. Revelation can not be partly true and partly false. God can not teach error. It comes therefore to this: was Christ God, and did He declare that there is a hell? All Christians believe that Christ is God. That Christ taught that there is a hell is as certain as that the Gospels are true. Yet there are some Christians who do not believe in hell. They say that God is too good to send anyone to hell. In the first place God sends no one to hell. God does everything to keep us from hell. Christ died on the cross in order to save us from hell. Anyone who goes to hell does so in spite of God's warnings.

Some people choose to believe only the agreeable things that Jesus taught. They make their own creed by selecting what is acceptable to them and rejecting the rest. Suppose they should do that with regard to the Constitution of the United States? Suppose they should swear to accept the benefits of the Constitution but not its obligations! The Government would not acknowledge them as citizens. Now this is precisely what some people do with regard to the teaching of Christ. They accept what is agreeable to them and reject what displeases them, like a citizen accepting the protection of government but refusing to pay taxes. But Christ did not propose His teaching, He imposed it. He spoke with authority. He spoke as God. God does not debate with man, He proclaims His truth and declares His will.

To-day, outside the Catholic Church and some of the denominations which are called old-fashioned, the doctrine of hell is not preached. Many so-called Christians rather pity those who are so weak-minded as to believe in hell. Every denomination which separated from the Catholic Church at the time of the so-called Reformation believed in hell. If it was true then, it is true now. If it was false then, their creed was false from the beginning and can not be the creed of Christ. This is as plain as that two plus two equal four.

Hell is as repugnant to Catholics as it is to others. Catholics do not believe in hell because they relish the doctrine, but because they believe in Christ. Catholics believe that all that Christ taught is divinely true. They believe in hell, not because they comprehend how the good God can declare such a doctrine, but because He has declared it. We know that God is good yet we see many things in life which we can not reconcile with His goodness. Because we can not square the evils of life with God's goodness we do not deny the evils.

We know that God is good because He has given us our mothers. We know that God is good because He has given us the beautiful flowers, and the green meadows, and the smiling valleys, and the cheerful sunlight, and the gorgeous sunsets, and the birds that sing and the crops that feed us. The heart of a mother proclaims the goodness of Him Who gave it. So we know that God is good.

Yet how reconcile the goodness of God with the misery of mankind? Famine, plague, earthquake, flood, seem to contradict a good God. Some are born cripples, some blind, some insane. How reconcile all this with the goodness of God? Go to a cancer hospital or a leper colony and then see if you are not asking yourself, "How does God allow it?" And, worst of all, moral evils: murder, theft, calumny, perjury, injustice! How can God be good and permit all this contamination? We—with our limited knowledge, and vision—can not reconcile God's goodness with the misery around us. But because we can not reconcile God's goodness with the evils of life we do not deny the evils.

Hell is repugnant to us. So are cancer and smallpox and rattlesnakes. Nevertheless cancer and smallpox and rattlesnakes abound. Because we dread smallpox we do not deny its existence, but take precautions against it. Death is repugnant, yet it is a fact. Hell is a fact, even though it be repugnant. God intends it to be repugnant. He wants it to be dreaded by us. The reason why vice is so rampant to-day is because hell is unfashionable. If with belief in hell people sometimes go astray what would the world be without the fear of hell? There are times in the life of the best of men when the fear of hell is the one thing that prevents sin.

Voltaire was once complimented by one of his disciples who wrote to him as follows: "I congratulate you, that at last you have convinced me that there is no hell." To which Voltaire replied: "Lucky man to be so convinced. I wish I could convince myself that there is no hell."

On the one hand is Christ Who solemnly and repeatedly declares that there is eternal chastisement for the unrepentant. On the other hand is the repugnance of man to this doctrine. Man willingly enough believes in heaven because God proclaims it. Why believe God's word that there is heaven and deny His word that there is hell? Some people are solicitous for God's goodness but not for His veracity. They say God is too good to punish, but they do not hesitate to say that He is not to be believed. If there is no hell Christ has declared what is false and has misled the world for centuries. Up to the sixteenth century all Christians believed in hell on the word of Christ. Was Christ's word true for a time only? Did Christ cease to be the Way, and the Truth and the Life (Jn. xiv. 6.) when men saw fit to deny His teaching? A man may go into a cellar at midday and close out the light, and then declare that it is midnight. But it is day, nevertheless. Christ has taught us that there is a hell. If we dread eternal punishment let us avoid it. We avoid leprosy. If Voltaire could not convince himself that there was no hell, it should be the part of a prudent man to take no chances.

A sceptic once said to a Christian: "I am thinking what a disappointment will be yours, Christian, when you find that there is no heaven." To which the Christian replied: "I am thinking what a shock will be yours, Sir Sceptic, when you find that there is a hell."

If there is no hell, what meaning has Redemption? If there is no hell, why is Christ called *Our Saviour?* If there is no hell, why did Christ say: "What does it profit a man, if he gain the whole world, and suffer the loss of his soul?" (Mt. xvi. 26.) If there is no hell why did Christ die on the Cross?

Deny hell if you will, but in doing so you proclaim that Christianity is false. It is Christ's word against your sentiments. Christ has said: "Heaven and earth shall pass away, but My word shall not pass away." (Mk. xiii. 31.) If you dread the thought of hell keep away from the path that leads to it. We do not play with rattlesnakes. Hell is as certain as God's word is true.

CHAPTER XVIII

INDULGENCES

IN the consideration of indulgences the most important thing is to have a right notion of what is meant by an indulgence. In order to have a correct idea of what an indulgence is, it is necessary to have a clear conception of what sin is.

What crime is against the State, that, only much more so, sin is against God. A crime is a violation of the laws of the State. Sin is a violation of the laws of God. As the majesty of God is infinitely greater than that of the State it is evident that sin is altogether a more serious matter than an offense against the State. Most offenses which are serious against the State are also sins as well as crimes, as, for instance, perjury, theft, libel, murder, etc.

If a citizen commit a crime against the State and be convicted three consequences follow. First of all he is disfranchised, then he loses his liberty, and finally he receives punishment by various prison penalties. A criminal who is disfranchised, can no longer have the privileges of citizenship when he returns to civil life. There are attached to crimes against the State therefore three penalties, namely: loss of citizenship, loss of liberty for a specified time, and the minor punishments of prison life.

Sin is an offense against God. By sin is meant the violation of God's law knowingly, deliberately, and freely. A person can not commit a serious or mortal sin unless he know he is doing what is seriously wrong and unless at the time of the act he be free to do it or not to do it. A mortal sin is a deliberate, willful and serious transgression of God's law. The consequences of a serious transgression of God's law are threefold. First the sinner loses God's friendship, secondly he loses his inheritance to eternal companionship with God in heaven, and thirdly he incurs the temporal chastisement which accompanies every sin.

The State, through its pardoning board may forgive a criminal, and remit entirely or partly the punishment of his crime. It may restore him to full citizenship, or it may restrict his civil rights. It may commute his term of imprisonment to a fine. Perhaps if people, who have deserved well of the State, petition in the criminal's behalf, special consideration will be shown him if he be rightly disposed, which otherwise would not be granted. Sometimes, after a criminal has been convicted, the judge instead of sentencing him to prison may put him on parole.

In all such favors shown the convicted, the State manifests indulgence towards them. The State, therefore, through its appointed agencies, shows consideration or indulgence to repentant criminals, either because of extenuating circumstances or on account of the petition of those who have done notable service for the State. Whenever a prison sentence is changed to a fine, or imprisonment, or replaced by parole, the State through its proper agency grants an indulgence. Whenever the Governor of a State grants a reprieve, or commutes the death sentence to life imprisonment, he grants an indulgence.

What the State does with regard to those who violate its laws, that God may do, and actually does with regard to those who violate His laws. God's mercy is over all His works. He desires not the death of the sinner but that the sinner repent and live eternally. Christ came for sinners. He said that not they who are well need the physician, but they who are ill. Those in sin are mortally ill of soul. Christ Who has said that the unrepentant sinner shall be banished forever from the kingdom of the blessed, has also said: "There shall be joy in heaven upon one sinner that doth penance." (Lk. xv. 7.)

God is the Judge of true repentance. He sees the heart. All the pardons and indulgences in the world avail nothing if the heart be not right. God's pardon and indulgence which are so generously bestowed on those who truly repent can not benefit the sinner who does not resolve in his heart to give up sin. Let this be understood above all else, that neither the sacramental pardon of confession, nor the indulgence which may be granted outside confession, are of any value unless the sinner be disposed to give up his sin. If some Christians abuse God's generosity by presuming on His mercy to commit sin with impunity, they are indicting themselves, not God's goodness.

Having said the above, by way of introduction to the subject of indulgences, let us now consider what is meant by an indulgence as understood in the language and practice of the Church of Christ. An indulgence is the remission, totally or partially, of the temporal chastisement due to sin after the guilt of sin has been remitted. An indulgence can never be received by one who is in the state of sin. An indulgence can only be imparted to one who is repentant.

An indulgence is a remission of chastisement outside the sacrament of Penance, since it may be gained by specified meritorious acts independent of confession, but always presupposing that the person in question is not in the state of sin. As the State delegates pardoning power to the Governor or a pardoning board, so Almighty God has delegated pardoning power to His divinely established Church.

While on earth Christ forgave sin and also the temporal chastisement due to sin. He forgave Magdalene and made her the companion of His blessed Mother. He forgave the thief on the cross and also granted him the complete remission of the temporal chastisement due to sin, for He said to the penitent criminal: "This day thou shalt be with Me in paradise." (Lk. xxiii. 43.) Thus Christ forgave this notorious sinner and granted him moreover a plenary indulgence. Not only that but He canonized the repented thief, declaring that in that very day he was to be in heaven, where only saints dwell with God and the angels. Who will limit God's mercy after this act of indulgence!

The power of forgiving sin and granting indulgence which Christ exercised, He conferred upon His Church. "All power is given Me in heaven and on earth. . . . As the Father hath sent Me, I also send you. . . . Whose sins you forgive they are forgiven. . . . Whatsoever thou shall loose upon earth shall be loosed also in heaven." (Mt. xxviii. 18. Jn. xx. 21. Mt. xvi. 19.) Thus did God delegate to His Church the power of forgiving sins and granting indulgence, somewhat the same as the State grants to its pardoning agency the power to pardon or to reprieve sentences.

The Church of Christ is the continuation of Christ's ministry. "He that heareth you, heareth Me. . . . Behold I am with you all days, even to the end of the world." (Lk. x. 16. Mt. xxviii. 20.) Christ established His Church to do what He Himself had done. "As the Father hath sent me, I also send you." (Jn. xx. 21.) This is the Charter of Christ's Church. Acting on her divine Charter the Church not only pronounces pardon on the repentant sinner in the sacrament of Penance, but also outside confession, commutes the chastisement ordinarily due to sin to works of piety and charity, if the sinner be rightly disposed and fulfill the prescribed conditions.

In the first ages of Christianity certain penances, called canonical, were customarily attached to sin. These penances were called canonical from the word canon which means rule or regulation. When an indulgence was granted in the early ages it was for the remission of these canonical penances which had been assigned as temporal chastisement for the sins committed. When these canonical public penances ceased for various reasons, the Church in granting indulgences retained the terms employed in these canonical penances. A sinner, for instance, might have received as canonical penance a chastisement which was to continue for thirty days, or a year, or a lifetime, according to the guilt. When an indulgence for thirty days or a year was granted, it did not mean that it remitted thirty days or a year of purgatorial punishment, but that it remitted that temporal chastisement which was assigned by those canonical penances. The Church retains the ancient forms of indulgences although she no longer ordinarily assigns public canonical penances.

Indulgences are either partial, which remit part of the temporal chastisement due to sin; or plenary which remit the chastisement entirely. When God forgave David his sin, He did so by the agency of the prophet Nathan. God seeing the repentant heart of David remitted the guilt and eternal consequences of his great sin, but not the temporal chastisement, as we know. God's dispensation in the New Testament has provided more abundant mercy for repentant sinners. By the agency of His Church He forgives sinners as He forgave David by the prophet Nathan. But besides the power of forgiveness He has also conferred upon His Church the dispensing power, by which in His name she may commute the chastisement of sins into works of charity and piety. "Whatsoever thou shalt loose upon earth shall be loosed also in heaven." (Mt. xvi. 19.)

Christ's Church has understood and exercised her dispensing and commuting power from the very beginning of Christianity. In virtue of Christ's merits and by His authority she grants indulgences to those rightly disposed. If a sinner be in earnest about his conversion, he has the assurance of Jesus Christ that the mercy shown him by the Church is ratified in heaven. This is why Catholics are desirous of gaining indulgences not only for themselves but also for their departed beloved ones. For by the communion of Saints proclaimed in the Apostles' Creed, the faithful on earth can help those who have gone before, and who are undergoing purification before they can enter the abode of the all-holy God.

Indulgences, rightly understood, give glory

to the merciful God and comfort to frail humanity. When we consider that no indulgence can be gained by one who is in the state of sin, we may realize what a powerful incentive to conversion, and what a strong motive to holiness is the Christian doctrine and practice of indulgences.

CHAPTER XIX

FREEMASONRY

IT is well known that the Catholic Church is opposed to Freemasonry. Indeed it is excommunication for a Catholic to be a Freemason. Freemasons know this. Parkinson, an illustrious Mason says: "The two systems of Romanism and Freemasonry are not only incompatible, but they are radically opposed to each other." (Freemason's Chronicle, 1884, II, 17.) This is so well understood that we are not surprised to know that Masons as a body do not want Catholics in their ranks. "We won't make a man a Freemason until we know that he isn't a Catholic." (Freemason's Chronicle, 1890, II, 347.)

Freemasonry is a very widespread organization, and it may well be that in certain localities and among certain groups these sentiments toward Catholicism and Catholics do not prevail. However, all that I shall say with regard to Freemasonry characterizes the order as it shows itself in its constitutions and as it has manifested itself in its activities. I have met Freemasons who have assured me that there was nothing in their organization which was in any way opposed to the Catholic Church. These were sincere men, and doubtless spoke from personal knowledge. Some of these men were high up in the order and respected it greatly. These men were converts to the Catholic faith. They left Freemasonry because they understood that they could not be Catholics and Freemasons.

In considering Freemasonry, we must keep in mind the distinction between the order and the individual. One may be opposed to the Republican or Democratic party and yet esteem the individual members of the party. In considering Freemasonry we have in mind the order as an order, its essential and practical attitude toward the Catholic Church. In the first place it is necessary to say that very few of the rank and file of Freemasonry are acquainted with the real purpose of the order. This may sound strange, considering the Freemasons are for the most part men of superior intelligence. It seems so strange that I feel I must give authority for the statement. "Brethren high in rank and office, are often unacquainted with the elementary principles of the science of Freemasonry." (Oliver, Theocratic Philosophy, 355.) "Masons may be fifty years masters of the Chair and yet not learn the secret of the Brotherhood." (Oliver, Hist. Landmarks, I, 11, 21.) There is no higher authority on Freemasonry than Oliver, himself a Freemason.

The fact that the real purpose and aim of the order is so little known to the generality of Masons explains why it is that Masons themselves, in all sincerity, will declare that the purpose of the order is mainly fraternal and philanthropic. However, we shall see for ourselves, by the clearest evidence, what the real purpose of the order is. The Catholic Church is the greatest encourager on earth of fraternalism and philanthropy. She is also the best informed organization in the world. Unless, in fact, Freemasonry was opposed to what she fundamentally stands for, she never would be opposed to it as she is. In point of fact Catholic Freemasonry existed for centuries as a benevolent and fraternal organization before the birth of the present non-Catholic Masonry. Catholic Freemasonry took its origin from the guilds of the middle ages. Stonemasons had their guilds as well as other crafts. Each local group had its own guild. Certain skilled masons used to travel from place to place wherever there was a Gothic cathedral in course of erection. These masons in coming to a new place had to be acknowledged by the local guild before they could practise their craft. For this purpose they carried with them certificates that they were qualified masons and free to work in any place. Hence they were called freemasons, not being restricted to a local guild. These freemasons formed a guild of their own, with a code of signs and passwords. All talk about the antiquity of Freemasonry is myth, pure and simple. Freemasonry, as it exists to-day, began with the foundation of the Grand Lodge of England, June 24, 1717. In the beginning it was just a social organization. By degrees it developed into its present form and purpose. Modern Freemasonry is not a continuation of the Catholic freemason guilds which preceded it. The Catholic guilds were formed by craftsmen who, as said previously, went from one city or country to another, wherever a Gothic cathedral was being erected, in order to help in its construction. On the decline of Gothic architecture Catholic Freemasonry ceased to exist, or rather was absorbed by local guilds. Freemasonry as it now exists is absolutely a non-Catholic foundation of the beginning of the eighteenth century. It was introduced into the United States about the year

1730, and subsequently into France, Germany, Italy, and Europe generally.

Why is the Catholic Church opposed to Freemasonry? The shortest and best answer is because Freemasonry is opposed to the Catholic Church. Even to some Freemasons this statement will come as a shock. But we must remember what was said previously by authoritative men of the order, that the rank and file of Masonry are ignorant of its real significance. Moreover, Masonry in this country and in England has not openly adopted the measures against the Catholic Church which have been employed by Freemasonry in France, Italy, and other Continental countries. In fact, English and American Freemasonry have endeavored to deny connection with the revolutionary and anti-religious Freemasonry of Continental Europe.

The activities of Continental Masonry became so revolutionary that they occasioned the following communication from the Registrator of the London Grand Lodge to the Grand Lodge of Massachusetts. "We feel that we in England are better apart from such people. Indeed Freemasonry is in such bad odor on the Continent of Europe, by reason of its being exploited by Socialists and Anarchists that we may have to break off relations with more of the

Grand Bodies who have forsaken our landmarks." (New Age, New York, 1909, I, 177.)

In proof that Masonry is unified the world over, let me quote a Past Grand Master, Clifford: "The absolute oneness of the craft is a glorious thought. Neither boundaries of States, nor vast oceans separate the Masonic fraternity. Everywhere it is one. There is no universal church, but there is a universal fraternity, Freemasonry." (Freemason's Chronicle, 1906, II, 132.)

Individual Masons and local fraternities may be sincere in disclaiming association with the dreadful doings of the order in other lands, but it is because they do not know what is going on among those who control the activities of their order.

Having demonstrated, from official and public sources, the brotherhood which exists among Freemasons the world over, let us see why the Catholic Church is opposed to the order, and excommunicates those of her subjects who join it. I shall make no charges of my own against Freemasonry, but shall let it speak for itself. Senator Delpech, President of the Grand Orient, in an address September 20th, 1902, said: "The triumph of the Galilean (Jesus Christ) has lasted twenty centuries. But now He dies in

His turn. The mysterious voice, announcing the death of Pan (to Julian the Apostate), to-day announces the death of the impostor God. Brother Masons, we rejoice to state that we are not without our share in this overthrow of the false prophets. The Romish Church, founded on the Galilean myth, began to decay rapidly from the very day on which the Masonic association was established." (Compte-rendu Gr. Or. de France, 1902, 381.) That is plain language and plain opposition to Christianity. Italian Masonry is even more radical than the French, and proclaims that it is supported by the Freemasonry of the world, and especially by the Masonic centers at Paris, Berlin, London, Madrid, Calcutta and Washington. ("Riv." 1842, 291; Gruber, "Mazzini" 215.)

In some countries, our own, for instance, and England, where public opinion does not countenance irreligion, Freemasonry does not disclose its attitude toward Christianity. But in very truth, the essence of Freemasonry is opposition to revealed religion. If its main assaults are against Catholicism it is because the Catholic Church is the main bulwark of Christianity. Freemasonry employs the symbols and the terminology of religion in order the better to carry out its purpose. As said previously, American and English Masonry among the rank and file are unacquainted with the real purpose of the order. They even praise Freemasonry as an upholder of religion, and quote their ritual to prove it. But the religion which Freemasonry upholds is the religion which ignores the revelation of Jesus Christ, and assails the doctrines which His divinely instituted Church proclaims. "The two systems of Romanism and Freemasonry are not only incompatible, but they are radically opposed to each other." (Freemason's Chronicle, 1884, II, 17.)

In time of war the soldiers in the ranks, and often commissioned officers, know little or nothing of the plans and purposes of their superior officers. They have no personal hostility to the soldiers of the enemy army, often fraternizing with them when occasion offers. Notwithstanding this, the two armies are opposed to each other, and the men in the ranks, without knowing the mind of the commanding general, are executing his commands and carrying out his purposes. It is against the enemy, as an organized opposition, and not against individual soldiers, that war is declared and fought. A government would condemn a subject as guilty of treason if he went over to the enemy ranks. This is what the Catholic Church does if one of her subjects joins the Freemasons. She knows, not from hearsay, but from official documents, and from actual hostilities, that Freemasonry, as an institution, is unequivocally and essentially opposed to her. She stands for revealed religion. Freemasonry ignores revelation, and in European countries openly employs all its resources to crush the one Church which upholds in its entirety the religion of Jesus Christ.

CHAPTER XX

ASH WEDNESDAY AND LENT

ASH Wednesday is so called because on this day the priest makes the sign of the cross with ashes on the forehead of the faithful. While doing so he pronounces these words: "Remember man thou art but dust and unto dust thou shalt return." These words remind us that although we must live in this world we must not live altogether for this world. The words of our poet Longfellow, come to mind with regard to the ceremony of Ash Wednesday:

"Life is real! Life is earnest!
And the grave is not its goal;
Dust thou art, to dust returnest,
Was not spoken of the soul."

"Dust thou art, and unto dust thou shalt return." (Gen. iii. 19.) are the words of Almighty God to Adam. God in so speaking reminded man that this present life is not to be his *chief* concern. The ceremony of receiving the ashes recalls the fact that man's perishable body must be his servant, not his master; that eternal life is the main purpose of man, not this passing life.

Ash Wednesday also marks the beginning of Lent. Lent is a period of forty days of fasting and abstinence. It is a period during which Christians seek to show God by deeds of penance that they are sorry for having offended Him. It is also a period during which, in a special manner, Christians endeavor to show Christ their gratitude for His redeeming sufferings. He, although without sin, endured besides other pangs a fast of forty days, in order to atone for our sins. Christians in imitation of Him, their Model and Leader, refrain at stated seasons from what is enjoyable.

Sacrifice is the language of love. It was by sacrifice, not by words only, that Christ manifested His love for us. It is by sacrifice rather than by words that we can best prove our love for Him. Not that God delights in the suffering or privation of His followers, but in the love which these inflictions indicate. A mother does not delight in the suffering of a child, yet if a mother learned that her son had deprived himself of a day's pleasure for her sake, she would surely rejoice,—not in his privation but for the proof of his love for her which is manifested.

Sacrifice is not only the language of love but of penance also. It is easy to say that we are sorry for our transgressions. Words are cheap. But if by deeds, which cost us the privation of what we greatly like, we express our sorrow for sin, we give substantial proof of our desire to atone and to repent. There are some people who say that the Church is cruel to impose fasting and other restrictions on the faithful. It all depends on what is the object of the restrictions. People continually impose on themselves greater privations than does the Church on the faithful. We all know what people suffer for fashion's sake. The physician of the body often prescribes a restricted diet for bodily health. The Physician of the Soul ordains penance for the eternal welfare of the soul. Catholics do not fast because they are in love with fasting, nor does the Church impose penance because she wants to inconvenience or pain her subjects. She is simply carrying out the directions and commands of her divine Founder, Who proclaimed: "Unless you do penance you shall all likewise perish." (Lk. xiii. 3.)

Christ made penance a condition of salvation. The Church ordains only public and sacramental penance. God commands, besides, personal penance on all those who have transgressed His holy law. This is why Christians offer to God, in satisfaction for their sins, the afflictions of life and in addition impose on themselves various mortifications. The Church, like a good and wise Mother, does not leave the practice of penance altogether to the fickleness and forgetfulness of her children, but assigns certain seasons and forms of penance to remind them of this sacred obligation. None of us can say with Christ: "Which of you shall convince Me of sin?" (Jn. viii. 46.) It is because Christ knew the heart of man that He said: "Bring forth therefore fruits worthy of penance." (Lk. iii. 8.) In the very beginning of His public mission Christ insisted on the need of penance: "Do penance, for the kingdom of God is at hand." (Mt. iv. 17.)

Penance, as commanded by Christ, is a virtue which includes sorrow for sin and the desire to atone for sin. David gives us an example of penance in his great act of contrition embodied in Psalm 50: "Miserere mei Deus." ("O God, have mercy on me.") He was not only sorry for his transgression of God's law, but bowed his head humbly to the dreadful chastisement which the prophet Nathan pronounced against him, when he declared that God would take from him his beloved child. True sorrow leads to self-chastisement, and we know from Scripture how David afflicted himself to the end of his days for his brief unfaithfulness to God's law. In this way he sought to expiate his sin.

Expiation consists of acts of penance offered up in order to atone for sin. Every sin is an act by which a rational being—in deed, if not in word—defies God. The sinner is one who instead of saying to God as Christ directs in the Lord's Prayer: "Thy will be done," says—at least by deed—"Not Thy will, but mine be done." Every sin is a choosing of some gratification which is against the law of God. Since by sin a man indulges in some unlawful pleasure, atonement requires that something of an unpleasant nature be suffered which will show that repentance is real.

Chastisement for sin takes principally one or other of three forms:

The first is the patient acceptance of the afflictions of life which Providence permits in our regard. A chastisement not of our own choosing is often a better atonement for sin than a penance of our own selection. Subtle self-love may inspire self-imposed penances. But self is absent in the afflictions which come to us unsought. Resignation to Providence in the trials of life, as an act of atonement for sin, is one of the most effective acts of penance that can be offered to God. To say from the heart: "Thy will be done," when the hand of sorrow or pain rests heavily upon us, is the best way to atone for having said, by deed, when sinning, "My will be done instead of Thine."

The second form of chastisement as a means of expiating our sins is to practise faithfully the penances enjoined by the Church,—God's representative on earth. Lenten restrictions—such as abstaining from certain kinds of food; curtailing our ordinary amount of food; and refraining from certain amusements—give us the opportunity of offering to God most acceptable satisfaction for our trespasses.

Finally, an excellent way of expiating our sins is to impose certain restrictions on ourselves as chastisement. Many Christians refrain from some favorite diversion during Lent. Some give up pleasant habits. Some deny themselves sweets and shows. In all such mortifications it must be borne in mind that the value of them in God's sight is the motive which inspires them. If they are offered to God in the right spirit they will not only draw down His forgiveness but also cancel the chastisement which follows every sin either here or hereafter.

Besides making expiation for sin, penance is

also a powerful means of sanctification. Good-will is what God values most. Penance is an excellent indication of good-will, particularly if it be practised in the right spirit. Penance reminds us that we have not here a lasting city. It impresses upon us, moreover, the fact of judgment, which is a strong incentive to do good and avoid evil. Above all it shows our Saviour that we wish to cooperate with Him for our eternal salvation.

Those acts of penance are most acceptable to God which manifest charity. Christ takes as done to Himself what we do unto others in His name. Kind words, which may cost us much under certain circumstances; kind deeds towards those whom we may consider not entitled to them; a helpful hand to a struggling brother; these and other such deeds of charity done as acts of expiation constitute penance which will not only satisfy for our sins but will render us very dear to our divine Lord. Christ Himself has said: "There shall be joy in heaven upon one sinner that doth penance." (Lk. xv. 7.) This means that penance makes us acceptable to God.

It is not the Church which has originated penance but her divine Founder. Christ proclaimed: "Do penance, for the kingdom of God is at hand." (Mt. iv. 17.) It was because God commanded His Church to preach penance that the apostles were so insistent on it. St. Peter exhorted his hearers to penance in these words: "Do penance, and be baptised every one of you in the name of Jesus Christ, for the remission of your sins." (Acts ii. 38.) St. Paul preached to Jew and Gentile "That they should do penance, and turn to God, doing works worthy of penance." (Acts xxvi. 20.) In writing to the Corinthians he states: "Now I am glad: not because you were made sorrowful but because you were made sorrowful unto penance." (II Cor. vii. 9.) In thus exhorting to penance the apostles were following the example of their Lord, Who had said: "Bring forth therefore fruits worthy of penance." (Lk. iii. 8.)

The holy season of Lent offers us the opportunity of bringing forth fruits worthy of penance. In doing so we know that we are doing what is acceptable to God and helpful for our everlasting welfare. Jesus said to the apostles: "Penance and remission of sins should be preached in His name, among all nations, beginning at Jerusalem." (Lk. xxiv. 47.) In prescribing the fast of Lent, therefore, the Catholic Church is fulfilling this mandate of her divine Founder.

CHAPTER XXI

EASTER

WHEN Christ rose from the dead on Easter morn He opened the gates of divine life to mankind. His Resurrection proclaimed that the grave was not the goal but starting point of man. Christ did not rise from the tomb for His own sake but for His followers. He rose as a victor over the grave, as a captain who had conquered death. A conqueror leads a host of followers in his triumphs, and Christ, the Conqueror of Death, is the Leader unto Eternal Life of all those who belong to the soldiers of the Cross.

Jesus had said that He came to give life. He was not speaking of his mortal life. His hearers already had mortal life, else He could not have addressed them. But He came to give them real life. The mortal life of man is rather death than life, since it leads inevitably to the grave. Man begins to die as soon as he is born. Sooner or later death will claim him. The life however which Christ came to give was a share in His own immortal life of glory. "To as many as receive Him He gives them the power to become the sons of God."

Christ's Resurrection was the final proof of His divine claims. Miracles are God's seal on a person or mission. The Resurrection of Christ was not only a great miracle, it was also a prophecy fulfilled. By the twofold seal of miracle and prophecy, therefore, Almighty God confirmed the mission and promises of Jesus Christ, His Only-begotten Son.

Christ's Resurrection is a pledge and guarantee of ours. This is why Easter is such a joyous feast. It proclaims that if we be followers of Christ here we shall hereafter be with Him in glory. If we are loyal to Him here we shall reign with Him hereafter.

The Resurrection was the final sign which Jesus gave in order to convince the world that He was truly the Son of God. It was because the apostles were convinced of the Resurrection that they consecrated their lives to preaching the religion of Christ. In the end they all sacrificed their lives for Him, rejoicing to witness to Him unto blood.

It was because Stephen believed in the Resurrection that he proclaimed that Christ was God, and died like his Master,—praying for his enemies who were stoning him to death. It was faith in the Resurrection which animated the martyrs who in millions went to dreadful torture and death rather than deny Christ. It was faith in the Resurrection which inspired countless men and women from every rank and condition of life to forsake all the attractions of the world in order to lead saintly lives as hermits, monks, confessors or virgins. It was faith in the Resurrection which animated the legion of holy missionaries in every age of the Church to leave home, friends and comfort in order to bring Christ into the lives of those who in pagan or savage lands sat in darkness and the shadow of death. It is faith in the Resurrection which to-day prompts that great army of priests and nuns who devote their lives at home and abroad to the service of the orphan, the aged, the ignorant and the suffering.

It is the Resurrection that forms the basis of Christian hope and animates the followers of Christ the world over. The Resurrection proclaimed louder than words that we have not here a lasting city. It taught mankind that the best use to make of life was to live for others for Christ's sake.

During His life Our Blessed Saviour frequently referred to His resurrection from the dead. The Jews knew that He had foretold this event, as is evident from the fact that after the Crucifixion they went to Pilate and asked him for a guard over Christ's tomb, stating that Jesus had declared that He was to rise from the dead. Pilate gave them the guard, and it is from their official report to the Jewish council that we have unique proof of the Resurrection. It is thus from hostile sources that the truth of the Resurrection was officially proclaimed.

Moreover for forty days after He rose from the tomb, Jesus associated with His disciples instructing and fortifying them for their future mission. Finally after promising them the Holy Ghost Who was to enlighten them from above He returned to His Heavenly Father, to prepare a place for them and for all those that love Him.

Christ's Resurrection is the surety of our resurrection. We, too, are to arise from the grave, either unto life everlasting with God, or everlasting banishment from God and happiness. How our resurrection will be accomplished we know not. But we do know, on the word of God, that it shall be effected. Round about us there are many things which typify the resurrection. The seed cast into the soil dies before it springs to new and increased life. Every winter we see the pall of death spread over the earth, only to give way under the warmth of Spring, to new life.

The vile worm of earth, the caterpillar, goes into its tomb a creeping thing of earth, to emerge after a time a beautiful winged creature of the air. As a worm it crawled on the ground and fed on the earth. As a butterfly it sails the air a lovely object to behold, and feeds on flowers and dainty foliage. So we, now creatures of earth, shall rise in due time to a glorious and immortal life, if in this life we be true to our divine Leader and Model. Where Christ is in glory there shall His loyal followers dwell with Him, sharing His divine life. Easter therefore is truly a joyous day. It is the day the Lord has glorified, a day which brings hope into the most dismal life, and brightness into the darkest outlook. This is the day the Lord hath made, let us rejoice in it, Alleluia!

A wayfarer on a rough and steep road does not mind the hardships of the way provided it lead to comfort, opulence and peace. The Resurrection of Christ is a divine guarantee that this life is the way to eternal life. It proclaims that no matter what be the vicissitudes and inequalities of our earthly pilgrimage, our heavenly Father's welcome awaits us at the end, if only we walk in the path which Our Saviour marked out. A miner from the wilds laden with gold does not mind the burden, nor the privations of the way as he proceeds back to civilization because he knows that his treasure will enable him to live in the enjoyment of all that his heart yearns for. We are pilgrims on the way to the country beyond the grave. The Resurrection assures us that the burdens and privations of life may be converted into gold for the kingdom of heaven. In God's providence they are the means of purchasing for us that home He has prepared for those only who love Him and who prove their love by fidelity under the various trials of life. If it was necessary for Christ our Leader and Model to suffer in order to enter into His glory, we should not be surprised if we, too, should be required to enter by the same gate. The Resurrection is the divine alchemy which transmutes the base metals of life into gold for God's kingdom.

It is because the Resurrection gives to Christians the divine assurance of immortal life beyond the grave that it has made them superior to persecution, misfortune, injustice and every other adversity. No wonder, then, that on this day there is joy upon earth. No wonder that Christians repeat with Holy Church: "This is the day which the Lord hath made, let us be glad and rejoice therein. Give praise to the Lord, for He is good, for His mercy endureth forever, Alleluia." Indeed God is good and deserves our praise, for He has made us the objects of His love. "They that shall be accounted worthy of that world and of the resurrection from the dead . . . can die no more, for they are equal to the angels and are the children of God, being the children of the Resurrection." (Lk. xx. 35.)

This divine assurance gives the followers of Christ that peace and joy which the world can neither give nor take away. Easter joy is based on God's promise that where He is in glory His lovers will be. We can all be lovers of the Risen Christ if we keep His commandments. "If you love Me keep My Commandments." We can be great lovers of Christ if for His sake we do what is specially pleasing to Him. "If thou wilt be perfect follow Me." We follow Christ whenever for His sake we do our best to help His cause, whether it be by our virtuous example, or by kindness in the home and outside, or by assistance to those who are sacrificing their lives for Him in missionary lands.

Sacrifice is the great proof of love, whether it be of our life or of our goods. Not that God needs us or our possessions. The earth is His and the fulness thereof. But He has given us life and placed His possessions in our hands that we may have the honor and merit of using them for His glory. It is an honor to be allowed to do something for an earthly monarch. It is a much greater honor to be allowed to do something for the King of Kings. The Resurrection is God's own guarantee that to them who live for Him He will grant a share in His own everlasting life of glory.

CHAPTER XXII

THE INDEX OF FORBIDDEN BOOKS

DURING the World War our government exercised strict censorship over the press. No statement nor book was allowed publication if it tended to encourage the enemy or to weaken our own morale. No book was permitted to enter our country if it assailed in any way the cause for which we were contending. So vigorously was this supervision exercised that not a few persons were imprisoned for its violation, for it is a well known fact that propaganda played a most important part in the Great War. We realized its efficacy when our air forces dropped down into the ranks of the German soldiers and into German cities the utterances of President Wilson. It is said that these did more damage than bombs. They certainly so weakened the morale of the people that the soldiers at the front found it impossible to continue their resistance. Propaganda may be good or evil. If it is true and serves a right purpose it is good. The preaching of the Gospel is propaganda. Christ Himself commissioned His apostles to engage in this propaganda: "Going therefore, teach ye all nations . . . teaching them to observe all things whatsoever I have commanded you." The various devices of spreading Bolshevism constitute propaganda of another kind—evil propaganda. It is clear that the government in debarring Bolshevist literature and Bolshevist speech is not doing so in order to repress liberty but to preserve liberty. Christ established a Church to continue His mission among mankind to the end of the world. He entrusted certain truths to her keeping which were to guide man to life everlasting. These truths are as unchangeable as God Who gave them. God can neither deceive nor be deceived. He does not have to learn by experience what is true but knows it always, since He is Truth itself and Eternal Wisdom. Consequently the doctrine He imparted to His Church is unchangeably true. Any teaching which contradicts Christ's teaching is false, no matter by whom or how uttered. Just as government was formulated to safeguard the lives, property and rights of subjects so the Church was established to safeguard the Faith of Christ and to transmit it unchanged to succeeding generations of mankind. Government aims at securing the temporal welfare of subjects, and to this end exercises supervision over whatever affects the peace and prosperity of the people. The mission of the Church is to procure the spiritual welfare of her children and to safeguard their eternal interests. It is her sacred and bounden duty to ward off by every right means whatever threatens the spiritual well-being of those who are confided to her care.

If her Founder or His doctrine be assailed she is as much obliged to defend them as our government is obligated to defend the Constitution. If anyone should publish a book which attacked the Constitution, government would not tolerate its circulation. This is the meaning of the Index as it is employed by the Church. Any book which attacks the divinity of Christ, or falsifies Him or His doctrine, is an assault on the Constitution of the Church. If Christ be not God and if His doctrine be not absolutely true the Church has no claims on mankind. If therefore a book be published which denies Christ's divinity or His claims or doctrine the Church would be false to her charge if she did not do all in her power to keep that book from poisoning her people. For such a book is veritable poison. Its nature is to destroy the life of Faith, that Faith which Christ gave His life to establish, and which if lived up to, will enable us to share in His divine life.

Faith is so precious that to preserve it the martyrs in millions gave up their lives in cruelest torments. Hence just as government protects citizens against treasonable literature so does the Church protect her subjects against whatever is destructive of Faith. What treason is in the State, heresy is in the Church. The State not only proceeds against traitors but also forbids the circulation of traitorous books. The Church likewise defends herself not only against heretics but also against heretical writings. Heretics she banishes from her communion, their writings she excludes from her people. Literature which assails Christ or His doctrine is destructive of Christian belief and conduct. What a plague is to physical life heretical writing is to spiritual life. Under forbidden books the Church includes every kind of literature that assails faith or pollutes morals. Any immoral book is heretical in the sense that it advocates what is opposed to Christ's doctrine which always inculcates morality. Eventually any writing which attacks Christ or His teaching results in a spiritual plague. This has been the history of every heresy and of every immoral doctrine. Hence the Church guards her children against heretical and immoral books as government guards her subjects against contagious disease. We know how careful the State is to stamp out smallpox or cholera or any other such contagion. Indeed it not only stamps out such plagues but takes every measure against their approach. Quarantine and other such precautions indicate the solicitude of the State for the protection of the people against what threatens their health or life.

Heretical and immoral books are as dangerous to the spiritual life and welfare of Christians as any contagious disease is to material well-being. Nearly all the great upheavals of society can be traced to vicious literature. When the mind is polluted by false doctrine or by vile literature it will not be long before the results of such contamination show themselves in action. Christ said that evil proceeds from within, —that from a corrupt heart there will arise vicious deeds. Evil or false ideas do not remain shut up in the mind but seek expression in conduct.

It is for this reason among others that the Church turns aside the stream of polluted and false literature from her subjects. Rather she bids them to keep away from the pollution. She brands the vile stuff and warns against it no matter how attractive it may appear. Some of the deadliest poisons seem harmless to the uninitiated. Moreover there are some drugs which eventually destroy mind and body yet which appear to be not only harmless but delectable. The average person, if he trusted to his own judgment with regard to some of these enticing drugs, would become their victim before he realized their dreadful nature. It is so with some literature. It seems to not a few that certain books are not only uncensurable but even highly commendable. This is because they exercise a certain fascination by their literary style or by the nature of the subject treated. But deadly poison may be kept in artistic containers. In point of fact it is the glamour of vice that constitutes its danger. If vice or deadly drugs could be known at sight for what they are they would cease to be a lure. But it is precisely because their evil consequences are hidden that they constitute a danger. We do not have to be told to keep away from a smallpox patient, or from a rattlesnake. Some of the vices result more detrimentally than disease or deadly reptile. These may indeed afflict the body even unto death itself, but certain vices kill body and mind, after causing indescribable torture to both. Vicious literature has even more baneful effects on the soul than harmful drugs have on the mind and body.

The Index is not an attempt to curtail intellectual freedom but a measure intended to preserve society in soundness of mind and body. Neither the individual nor society will suffer intellectually or morally by keeping away from the pernicious and polluted stream of literature which is banned by the Index. Those who object to the Index as a curtailment of personal freedom must remember that in the wisest and most liberal civil states personal freedom does not entitle citizens to be a law unto themselves. The only person who claims unlimited freedom is either a criminal or a madman.

CHAPTER XXIII

INTOLERANCE

INTOLERANCE, as generally understood, is a state of mind which prevents people from dealing reasonably with those who differ with them. It manifests itself especially in racial, political and religious matters. Intolerance can go so far as to make a person a fanatic or even insane. Intolerance is always a sign of a mind which is narrow or limited. It causes a person to see things from one viewpoint only, and mostly from a wrong viewpoint at that.

A well-educated person is seldom intolerant. A well-educated person may condemn persons or things, but always reasonably—that is, for just cause. The intolerant person is one who judges or discriminates against others unreasonably or without justification. Mostly, intolerance comes from ignorance or environment, which leads persons to take for granted certain things which have no existence in fact, or which have been distorted. Many people who are violently intolerant in youth, become very tolerant as they mature, and learn from experience or education that they were under mistaken notions earlier in life. Education is the best remedy for intolerance, provided the education be right.

When we speak of intolerance we ordinarily refer to a prejudiced mind. Intolerance makes one judge and act not on reason but on sentiment. It leads a person to shape his policy by his likes or dislikes. We are drawn to some people and repelled from others. But although we may not be able to control our likes or dislikes, we are able to prevent them from influencing us wrongfully.

Intolerance causes injustice since it ordinarily makes people refuse to give others their rights. For instance, citizens of the United States have certain constitutional rights. To seek to deprive any class of citizens of their rights because of dislike of them personally or racially is to act unjustly and unreasonably toward them. If individual citizens be not entitled to the rights of citizenship there are lawful means of disfranchising them. But to seek to deprive of their constitutional rights a group of citizens or a race because of dislike of them would be the same as refusing to pay people their wages because we dislike them.

If we do not like people we are not obliged to associate with them. If a certain class in a community use unfair business methods we are not obliged to deal with them. That is not intolerance. Intolerance means unreasonable discrimination. To discriminate against those who are brazenly vulgar or notably dishonest is not unreasonable. At times self-protection demands that offenders be brought to a sense of decency and fair-dealing by refusing fellowship with them. We cannot help our likes or dislikes. Nor can we help feeling disgust with disgusting people, nor contempt for those who are dishonest.

To condemn what is wrong is not intolerance. Christ was the most just and charitable person that this world has known; yet He flayed the Scribes and Pharisees for their duplicity and dishonesty. Tolerance does not mean that we should be indifferent to, or encourage those who defy or ignore the ethics of business or social life. If certain persons take advantage of laws and customs which were instituted by honorable people for public welfare, these offenders should be dealt with in such a way that while their rights would not be infringed upon, they would nevertheless realize that it does not pay to outrage fair-dealing and the proprieties of life.

It is not intolerance if people bring discrimination upon themselves, by insolent manners and sharp business practices. They are not victims of intolerance who bring just condemnation on themselves. Those who outrage the conventionalities and rights of honest and decent people can not expect to be on the same footing with those who respect the rights of others and the decencies of life.

If an element of the community be identified with practices of this kind, and does not frown upon such unethical and criminal practices, it should not be surprised that as a body it suffers in the esteem of the public and meets with just discrimination. Such an attitude of the public towards vulgarity and dishonesty is not intolerance but self-preservation. Intolerance, as said previously, is a frame of mind which leads people to act without justification. The public, as well as individuals, would be at the mercy of the vulgar and unscrupulous if there were no disapproval or condemnation of flagrant vulgarity and calculated dishonesty.

Oftentimes insolent and ill-mannered people consider themselves persecuted when they are only meeting with their deserts. But always such condemnation should be free from intolerance. The rights, even of the repulsive and crafty should not be ignored. Injustice is not remedied by injustice. But it is not injustice nor intolerance to condemn those who employ sharp business methods which strain the law and take unfair advantage of honest competitors.

Tolerance by no means implies that we approve of what is shocking, but that we do not allow our repugnance to influence us unjustly. Intolerance always implies unreasonableness or injustice. This leads to another phase of the matter.

There is intolerance and intolerance. There is an intolerance which is not unreasonable. There is such a thing as proper intolerance. Intolerance of certain things is not only right but necessary. We must be intolerant of evil. We must be intolerant of error. We must be intolerant of injustice. Intolerance under certain circumstances is the highest virtue. A good woman will tolerate no reflection on her honor. An upright man will tolerate no charge against his honesty. Our government will tolerate no trifling with the Constitution.

But except where there is question of evil or injustice, tolerance is a mark of good breeding and of real Christianity. The more true a man's religious convictions, the greater is his virtue of tolerance toward those who differ with him.

Tolerance must not be taken for indifference. Religious indifference makes one care little or nothing for what others believe. But that is not the virtue of tolerance. Religious tolerance means that although a person may be absolutely convinced that he has the truth, and is willing to die in its defense, he nevertheless, for the love of God, shows forbearance towards those whom he holds to be in error. God Himself gives us an example of his tolerance, since He allows the wheat and tares to grow side by side, and permits the sun to shine on just and sinners alike. Yet God so hates sin that He gave His life on the Cross to atone for it and to prevent it.

Intolerant people are hated. They stand in their own way. Their power for doing good is shackled. Tolerant people are loved, and in the end accomplish most good. Tolerance, when practised by those who have no religion, is a natural virtue, very beautiful and very admirable. When practised as a supernatural virtue, that is for the love of God Who so loved us, it becomes a very meritorious act of religion. Very often intolerant people think they are virtuous when they are simply stubborn or narrow. It is easy to be intolerant, difficult to be tolerant. Tolerance implies patience, unselfishness, and due regard for the feelings and traditions of others.

The most tolerant Catholics are the most devout Catholics. The present Supreme Pontiff is proof of this. Although condemning the anarchy and irreligion of the Russian Bolshevik régime, he was nevertheless one of the first and most magnanimous in sending relief to the distressed Russians, regardless of creed. The Pope would readily sacrifice his very life for the Faith, but at the same time he leaves individual private conscience to God. God has not asked His followers to pass judgment on others, but He has commanded them to love their neighbor. Cardinal Mercier was another example of magnanimous tolerance.

In our country, where there are so many various creeds and races, anybody or anything that is prejudicial to religious tolerance is a menace to true citizenship. Since the right to one's religious convictions is conceded by modern government, it follows that the State must allow her citizens to worship God as they wish, provided that worship does not conflict with the just laws of the country. Hence the State must tolerate the various religions which her subjects adhere to.

In the United States, where religious freedom

is guaranteed by the Constitution, every cult has equal rights before the law. Our Government has always respected the religious convictions of her variegated population. For any citizen or group of citizens to attempt to infringe on this constitutional freedom of worship is paramount to treason. The glory of our country has been respect for law and order. To stir up religious strife, directly or indirectly, is to undermine the very basis of peace and welfare. If a man does not respect his conscience he is not going to respect government. Intolerance assails a man for respecting his conscience. Religious intolerance thus attacks the firmest basis and support of the State.

By all means let us uphold truth and oppose error. But let us also leave the individual conscience to the judgment of God. That is what Christ did. That is what we must do if we would be His true followers.

CHAPTER XXIV

THE ROMAN QUESTION

RECENTLY it was announced that there were hopes of an early settlement of the Roman Question. For nearly sixty years what is termed *the Roman Question* has been a matter of deep concern to the kingdom of Italy and to the Papacy. Until this question is settled it is felt that neither Italy nor the Papacy will be able to accomplish satisfactorily its noble aims.

Just what is the Roman Question? It is one of the most delicate problems that ever confronted a government. If Italy were dealing with an outside state or government there would be no problem such as the Roman Question. The matter would be settled by the surrender of one party or the other, either by force of arms or arbitration. But the Papacy is not an outside government. It is not a hostile government. The Papacy is devotedly attached to Italy; and the Italians, as a people, are devoted to the Papacy. This is what constitutes the problem known as the Roman Question. The Italian Government and the Papacy, neither at enmity with the other, are, nevertheless, at what seems to be an impassé.

The problem is this: the Italians want a united Italy, which they hold to be incompatible with the territorial claims of the Papacy. The Papacy will not submit to being the subject of any temporal government. The Papacy, as the head of the Universal Church, must not belong to any one state. As sovereign ruler of the Universal Church the Pope must be unattached. The only way he can be unattached is to be a sovereign in his own right. This demands territorial independence. And this is just what the Italian Government has not seen its way to grant, because it seems to conflict with a united Italy.

If the Italian Government were hostile to the Papacy there would be no Roman Question. On the other hand if the Catholic Church were not universal there might be no Roman Question. But since the Italian Government is not hostile to the Papacy, and since the Catholic Church is world-wide—attached to no nation, the problem arises how to settle the question without detriment to Italian unity, and also without destroying the sovereign independence of the Papacy. It is because both sides to the problem are friendly that we have the Roman Question. If the Italian Government were not friendly to the Papacy there would be no Roman Question for the Government would override or ignore the Papacy. But this is just what the Government does not want to do.

The crux of the whole matter, therefore, is this: a friendly Government wants to respect the rights of the Papacy but does not see its way to doing so consistent with national unity. It may be said: why does not the Pope meet the Government half-way. There is no half-way. The Pope is either independent or not. If he is independent he must have sovereign rights. If he is not independent he may at any time in important matters be regarded by the world at large as the creature of the Government of which he is a resident. If the Catholic Church were national or local this might not be an obstacle, but it is an obstacle to a Church whose jurisdiction is world-wide, embracing every nation and people under the sun.

To this it may be replied that in the first three centuries the Papacy was subject to the Roman Empire. Yes; and during the first three centuries the Pope was so hampered that it was only the power of God that enabled him to rule over the Church. Besides, at that time the Roman Empire was virtually the Western World. To-day, when there are numbers of independent and powerful nations, the citizens of one nation are suspicious of those of another.

Again, it may be objected, since the loss of temporal power the Papacy has gained rather than lost in prestige and power. By a combination of circumstances this is true. But these circumstances are conditional, and may at any moment change. Up to the present the Italian Government has been so desirous of placating the Papacy, that neither king nor parliament has interfered with the Pope's international activities. The present position of the Papacy depends entirely on the continuance of Italian good-will, which at any time, under an unfriendly Government, may become hostile and dreadfully hamper the activities and impartiality of the reigning Pontiff.

If the Church were not for all time as well as for all the world she might be satisfied with temporal advantages. But since she is for all time as well as for all people she has to defend her rights. The Pope, as Sovereign Pontiff, must indeed be sovereign if he is to discharge his world duties properly. To-day he is in the enjoyment of quasi-sovereign rights, only by the favor of a well-disposed Government. He can not be a sovereign if he be a subject. To-day all the privileges of independence which he enjoys are favors granted him by a favorably-disposed people.

By the nature of his office he must be Sovereign Pontiff, subject to no earthly power for the necessary prerogatives for the discharge of his world-wide mission. But as the world is constituted it is impossible to be a sovereign without territorial independence. No matter how great and dignified a person may be he can not be a sovereign and at the same time a subject. It is because the Pope is the Sovereign Pontiff of the world-Church that he refuses the compromises and guarantees of the Italian Government. For no matter how generous be the guarantees of the Italian Government—and they are very generous—they leave him nevertheless an Italian subject. Moreover, generous as are the guarantees they may be withdrawn any day.

The Roman Question therefore reduces itself to this. The Italian people and Government want a united Italy. They also want to give the Papacy its rights, but do not see how they can do so without infringing on Italy's territorial unity. The Papacy wants Italy as well as every other country to be in the full enjoyment of its national rights but not at the expense of injustice to the rights of others.

God in the course of time providentially endowed the Papacy with territorial independence. No country in the world had such just rights to territorial sovereignty as the Papacy, and no government ever employed sovereignty so disinterestedly for the welfare of mankind as did the Papal. The Italian desire for national unity engendered the Revolution which in 1870 seized the unprotected Papal States in order to incorporate them with united Italy. The leaders of this movement realized that they were despoiling the Sovereign Pontiff of his sovereignty which was the oldest and most lawfully established in Europe or the world. In order to make some attempt at recompensing him for the seizure they drew up the Law of Guarantees for the Papacy. These guarantees were exceedingly generous, granting the Pope everything in money and protection except sovereignty. While they showed in a measure the good-will of the Italian Government, they were also evidence that the new government knew that it had wrongfully deprived the Pontiff of his rights. If it were not well disposed to the Papacy it could have seized the Papal States without any attempt at reconciliation or rectification whatever.

On Italy's part the Roman Question is the problem how to reconcile loyalty to the Papacy with a territorially united Italy. On the Pope's part the problem is how to maintain his sovereign rights against a Government and people that love and revere him. This is the problem that has engaged Italy, both Quirinal and Vatican, for the past half century. As said in the beginning of this article it now seems that there are hopes of an early settlement of the Roman Question. With so much good-will on both sides it should seem possible and feasible to adjust matters to the satisfaction of both sides.

The Pope on his part is willing to make every sacrifice and concession short of sovereignty. It may be asked why is the Pope not content to leave matters as they are, since under present conditions the Papacy is so highly revered throughout the world. The reason is that his present position is that of tolerance. It depends altogether on the domestic Italian laws which may be altered at any time. But if the Pope have territorial rights he will be a sovereign and will thus be protected by international law, and not be at the mercy of an individual nation. Switzerland is small and unarmed yet her sovereignty is secure by reason of international law.

The Pope in his friendly desire to settle the

Roman Question is willing to take a minimum of territory to satisfy his claim. The Italian Government also seems to realize that the despoiled Sovereign Pontiff is entitled to sovereignty, and of late has come to the conclusion that Italian unity would not be impaired by a limited territorial sovereignty of the Holy Father. With so much good-will on both sides it seems that a good understanding is not far off, and with it the end of the Roman Question.

CHAPTER XXV

THE POPE

SOMETIMES persons are heard to remark that there is too much pomp and circumstance about the Pope. They assert that the Supreme Pontiff presents a strange contrast to the meek and humble Founder of Christianity. Such persons forget that Christ's followers consisted of a handful of adherents, while the Church of which He was the tiny seed has developed into that wonderful organization which extends over the whole world and whose adherents number hundreds of millions.

The word *pope* comes from the Latin *papa,* which was derived from the Greek *papas* meaning *father*. Whenever the term *Pope* is now used it is always understood to mean the Holy Father of all Christendom.

Christ Himself constituted the Pope, in the person of Peter, the visible head of His Church. "And I say to thee: That thou art Peter [a rock]; and upon this rock I will build My Church, and the gates of hell shall not prevail against it. And I will give to thee the keys of the kingdom of heaven. And whatsoever thou shalt bind on earth, it shall be bound also in heaven: and whatsoever thou shalt loose on earth, it shall be loosed also in heaven." (Mt. xvi. 18, 19.) By these words Christ made Peter the foundation on which His Church was to rest. In all nations *the key* is the symbol of authority. By giving the power of the keys of His kingdom to Peter, Christ clothed him with authority to rule over His Church.

Furthermore, Christ promised to be with Peter as head of the Church to the end of the world. Hence He was speaking to the apostle in his official capacity as supreme visible head. The office was to last to the end of time. Peter and the other apostles lived only a few years, more or less. But the Church and its official visible head were to continue until the consummation of the world. The Church without a head would be like a headless body, and not the living organization instituted by Christ for perpetual life. Hence the successor of Peter, the visible head of the Church, is called the Vicar of Christ. *Vicar* means *one who acts in the person of another.*

In consequence of the world-wide existence of the Church and of her marvelous unity there is need of vast and intricate organization. Christ's Church in His own day consisted of Himself and His few disciples. Simplicity was, accordingly, not only possible but necessary. Today His Church is the largest corporate society in the world. The United States Government at Washington is now vastly different from what it was when our first president was in office. No one would expect the great machinery of our government to be as simple now as it was in the early days of the Republic. The Catholic Church is far more extensive and has more subjects than the United States Government.

In the Church we have first of all the parish, comprising the faithful people and their pastor. The pastor receives his commission from his bishop, just as a captain does from army headquarters. The bishop, in turn, receives his commission from the Pope, just as a general receives his from the Commander-in-Chief. A priest is ordained by the bishop; the bishop is consecrated by the designation of the Supreme Pontiff. By means of bishop and priest, therefore, the Pope is in close association with the hundreds of millions who constitute the flock of which he is chief visible shepherd.

In order to carry on the spiritual work of Christ's kingdom on earth there is need, therefore, of a vast and intricate machinery of administration. This administration of the Church is centered in what is called the Vatican—the Pope's governmental headquarters. Here is transacted a variety and bulk of business that is staggering in its proportions. Every quarter of the globe is in close communication with this central bureau of affairs. The work is so vast and so delicate that it is assigned to various commissions presided over by high dignitaries of the Church, usually Cardinals. The Cardinals may be called the Pope's Cabinet. Every important question that arises is submitted to them for deliberation and advice.

As the Catholic Church is active in every nation of the world, and as various questions arise between Church and State and between bishop and priest, and even between priest and people, and sometimes among the faithful themselves, it is evident that the Vatican is one of the vastest administrations in the world. With vast and intricate administrations there is associated necessarily a great deal of formality. This results in what some are pleased to call the pomp of the papal court. As well expect the Church to go back to the Catacombs as to return to the primitive simplicity of apostolic times.

Why, it may be asked of Protestants, should

they build cathedrals like that of St. John the Divine since the apostles had only the Catacombs as a place of worship? The Catholic answer is that nothing is too good for the Lord. In the early ages, when Christians were obliged to worship as best they could, they realized that any place of worship was better than none at all. Hence a private house or an underground passage of the Catacombs frequently served as a Christian temple. But when persecution ceased and the Church could worship God openly, she felt that God should have a dwelling in some way worthy of Him. At least she considered that God's dwelling should not be inferior to man's. And so under the Christian emperors there arose those wonderful basilicas which were the admiration of Christendom.

Besides having regard for God's dwelling, it was felt that there should be regard for God's Vicar. Hence, when the Roman Empire became Christian, the Pope, the visible head of Christendom, was regarded with the respect and reverence which became the representative of Christ. Christian emperors and Christian people desired to have their Supreme Pastor in a position of dignity and honor. It was the office that was honored, not the individual. Christ's Vicar was, by his official position, the most sacred and exalted personage in the world. Christ, though born in a stable, did not live there all His life. His Vicar, in the lifetime of St. Peter, dwelt, as it were, in a stable.

Christ is content with a hut as a dwelling for His Eucharistic presence, if a hut is the best that man can give Him. But when His followers are in a position to build Him a temple more worthy of Him, He certainly is not pleased to see them more solicitous for a dwelling for man than for Himself. Christians, knowing this, have always striven that their best in architecture and art should be dedicated to the Lord. Hence we behold the wonderful cathedrals of Christendom, the expression of Catholic faith and devotion to their Sacramental Lord.

So likewise in honoring Christ's Vicar Christians felt they were honoring Christ Himself. As soon, therefore, as the Church rose from the Catacombs the faithful began to surround the person of the Pope with tokens of respect, reverence, and loyalty. Gradually the Pope became the most revered personage in Christendom, as was right, seeing that he was Christ's Vicegerent. Emperors, in order to honor him and to facilitate his work, conferred on him donations of temporal domains. This necessitated civil administration, which, by degrees, eventuated in what is termed the temporal power of the Pope. We see something similar to this in the Trinity Corporation of the Episcopal Church of New York City. Non-Catholics who question the temporal power of the Pope make no question of the temporal power of the rector of Trinity Church of New York, and hundreds of similar instances.

Non-Catholics who speak of the simplicity of Christ in contrast with the pomp of the Pope, might well turn their attention to the pomp and possessions of the Episcopalian Hierarchy in England and elsewhere, and of the gorgeous temples erected to divine worship. If non-Catholic Churches have no Vatican it is because they have no corporate unity. If the non-Catholic Churches were a unified organization like the Catholic Church there would soon be evident the need of an institution similar to that of the Vatican. But as they have no corporate unity in the true sense, they have no need of headquarters and all the administrative offices and formality such an establishment implies.

It may be said that the need of a central bureau for the administration of spiritual matters is understandable, but that Rome is immersed in material affairs. The best reply to this is that if an ordinary rector of a non-Catholic

Church finds himself taken up considerably with the material affairs of his parish, what must be the needs of a world-wide Church administration? The Church of Christ is spiritual in the sense that it serves the spirit of man and employs spiritual means of grace, but the agencies are material. Men, not angels, are the ministers of God's sacraments. A Church which has to deal with literally hundreds of thousands of clergymen the world over must necessarily have a stupendous administration of a material nature.

All this seems clear and reasonable, it may be said, but why does the Pope assume royal state and pomp? The Pope, as the head of the largest corporate society in the world, is a most important personage. An Episcopalian bishop, who is head of a single diocese only, and whose office is spiritual not temporal, is clothed, nevertheless, with considerable dignity. It is most reasonable that the Pope, who is Bishop of bishops, should also be clothed with corresponding dignity.

To-day the Papacy is the most benign and most respected authority in the world. Considered merely as a personage, leaving out the matter of religion altogether, there is no more highly esteemed ruler in the world than the present Sovereign Pontiff. The Catholic Church may well be proud of her visible head, and Catholics the world over may be grateful that their Holy Father is such an exalted personage in Christendom.

THE END